COLLECTING
POLITICAL
MEMORABILIA

Richard Friz

HOUSE OF COLLECTIBLES

NEW YORK

House of Collectibles and colophon are registered trademarks of Random House, Inc.

RANDOM HOUSE is a registered trademark of Random House, Inc.

This book is available for special discounts for bulk purchases for sales promotions or premiums. Special editions, including personalized covers, excerpts of existing books, and corporate imprints, can be created in large quantities for special needs. For more information, write to Special Markets/ Premium Sales, 1745 Broadway, MD 6-2, New York, NY, 10019 or e-mail specialmarkets@randomhouse.com.

Please address inquiries about electronic licensing of reference products for use on a network, in software or on CD-ROM to the Subsidiary Rights Department, Random House Reference, fax 212-572-6003.

Visit the Random House Web site: www.randomhouse.com

Library of Congress Cataloging-in-Publication Data is available.

First Edition

0 9 8 7 6 5 4 3 2 1

May 2004

ISBN: 0-375-72089-8

CONTENTS

INTRODUCTION

Some observers have called the American presidential campaign an incredible national popularity contest. Harry Truman called it "our four year annual spasm." To many of us, it's a time of rejuvenation and reaffirmation, the thrill of being immersed in a truly fascinating pursuit of that quintessential of political artifacts—the pinback button.

The virtue of button collecting is that it can be approached from so many different angles. These tiny snippets reveal tidbits of history, and as such, are far more entertaining than those often dry tomes that were required reading back in our school days. We've often thought that if today's crop of presidential hopefuls took the time to study political buttons and their brief but succinct messages, they could avoid many of the pitfalls of our forebears. For example, one lesson that becomes readily apparent—negative campaigns almost always bring negative results.

If it's aesthetics that cause the adrenaline to flow, look no further than the hobby's "Golden Era," which blossomed in all its full color vibrancy over a century ago. The use of brilliant golds (almost like gold lamé) is alas, a legacy of the past. The attention to detail, the elaborate free-flowing designs are like artist's miniatures.

We usually caution new or would-be collectors not to look upon campaign buttons as a nest-egg that will pay big dividends. (*See:* "Don't Be Investment Obsessed," p. 11) Buttons lack liquidity, unlike say, an incredible rarity like a Double Eagle silver coin or a Fabergé egg that stands to be resold in one swift rap of the gavel. If you collect what you like, however, with discrimination, if you build up your button portfolio through reputable sources, the chances are excellent that your collection will appreciate in value over time.

There are purists in the hobby who are concerned that political parties today have shunted the pin-back buttons from starring roles to bit players. Politicos prefer to divert untold millions to television commercials, telephone blitzes, and the Internet. Yet no matter how intensely TV political spots go for the jugular, how clever or convincing they might be, you cannot hold a sound bite in your hand, and marvel at how it has survived the ravages of time, or ponder on whose lapel or blouse it was once proudly displayed. Only a political button can arouse that kind of personal emotion.

ABBREVIATIONS USED IN THIS BOOK

Political Parties

A	American Party
AF	Anti-Federalist Party
AM	Anti-Masonic Party
CU	Constitution Party
D	Democratic Party
DN	Northern Democrat Party
DR	Democrat Republican Party
SD	Southern Democratic Party
F	Federalist Party
I	Independent Party
ID	Independent Democrat Party
NR	National Republican Party
P	Populist Party
PG	Progressive Party
R	Republican Party
STR	States Rights Democratic Party
W	Whig Party

Button Color Abbreviations

r w b	red, white, and blue
blk, w	black and white

blk	black
cr	Cream
g	Green
gld	Gold
y	Yellow
o	Orange
bn	brown
p	Pink
s	Silver
multicolor	any combination of five or more colors.

Basic Button Sizes

$7/8$ **inch**

$1\frac{1}{4}$ **inch**

$1\frac{1}{2}$ **inch**

$1\frac{3}{4}$ **inch**

2 inch

$2\frac{1}{2}$ **inch**

3 inch

INTRODUCTION TO POLITICAL MEMORABILIA COLLECTING

1

SOME HISTORY

The manic scramble for political memorabilia, almost a reflex action with countless Americans, could well have been triggered as early as 1789 when the first metal "GW" Washington inauguration and clothing buttons were struck.

Because the two-party system was nonexistent until the 1824 Andrew Jackson era, early artifacts tended to be commemorative or memorial in nature. Ceramic pitchers, mugs and platters were invariably English, French and German imports. A smattering of textile and paper items are known for the Founding Fathers, but opportunities are limited and prices are often extemely high.

In the Jacksonian age, brass medalets were introduced, and in later campaigns came an inundation of medals and medalets, shell badges, mechanical pins, sewing boxes, snuff boxes, flasks, ribbons, sulphides and paper (popularly classified as ephemera).

William Henry Harrison's 1840 "Tippecanoe and Tyler Too, log cabin and hard cider" campaign created an unprecedented wealth of bandanas, ribbons, medalets, campaign flags, noisemakers, and ceramics, which Roger A. Fisher categorizes "as the material culture of Presidential campaigns."*

Innovations in later campaigns included Currier & Ives jugate lithographs of candidates, figural canes, tobacco-related accessories, and razors. In 1860, ferrotype portrait badges were introduced; cardboard portrait badges followed in 1864. Other novelties included arcade torches, lanterns, lapel studs, stickpins, mirrors, and ingenuous mechanical devices.

The actual purposeful collecting of political memorabilia in general, or campaign items specifically, has its origins in the late 1860s following the assassination of Abraham Lincoln. An almost morbid preoccupation with memorial items ensued.

Politics, as opposed to baseball and football, was then the national pastime. Commercial lithographers and engravers produced single-sheet political prints (many of them memorial in nature) that soon lined the parlors of Victorian homes. Daguerreotypes, ambrotypes and cartes de visites were lovingly collected and showcased in albums.

Another departure from predictable electioneering mementos took place in the late 1880s with "the battle of the bandannas."

Ironically, it was not until the late 19th century, some 35 years following Lincoln's death, that New York City's Grolier Club exhibited a retrospective of Lincoln lithographs.

A handful of affluent collectors had quietly amassed all manner of Lincolniana by that time, and eventually, their vast, priceless collections were bequeathed to the Na-

*Fisher's *Tippecanoe & Tyler Too,* published by University of Illinois Press in 1988, ranks as the definitive sourcebook on the subject.

tional Archives, the Library of Congress, the Smithsonian, and other hallowed institutions for all to view and enjoy.

Robert T. King's *Lincoln in Numismatics*, listing over 1,000 medalia issues honoring Abraham Lincoln, appeared in February, 1924. Two other volumes that had an impact on the hobby as we know it today were Bessie M. Lindsey's *American Historical Glass* in 1948 and J. Doyle DeWitt's *A Century of Campaign Buttons* in 1959.

Further impetus for collecting political memorabilia came, much, much later. Unlike coin and stamp catalogs, which have been around for at least a century, the first political button catalogs did not appear until the 1960s and 70s.

Epic, large-scale international events, notably the U.S. Centennial Exposition in 1876 in Philadelphia and the Columbian Exposition in Chicago in 1892, and the St. Louis World's Fair of 1904, played pivotal roles in rekindling our patriotic spirit. Chromolithograph posters, prints, trading cards, and postal cards made an auspicious debut. Ceramics, glassware, and textile souvenirs abounded and were merchandised to honor our presidents, statesmen and military heroes of the past. The collecting mania continues unabated, stimulated by significant anniversaries and what pundit H. L. Mencken called "America's quadrennial circus," the national elections—exercises in sustained silliness and rhetorical overkill, a mixture of serious purpose with a large dash of hokum."

The APIC Saga

In 1945, just as World War II was winding down, the American Political Items Collectors, the first and foremost organization of its kind in the hobby, was founded. The APIC was initiated and nurtured through its first 15 years as members corresponded by mail. U. I. "Chick" Harris, one of the founding members and APIC historian relates:

"Monroe D. Ray, then living in Belmont, New York, had been putting on displays of his items at banks and other businesses throughout upstate New York . . . attracted the attention of newspapers and *Hobbies* magazine. *Hobbies* then forwarded letters from other political collectors to Monroe, allowing him to develop correspondence with many of them, resulting in APIC. Originated by Monroe and named by Joe Fuld of Hailey, Idaho. Other charter members were John W. Barkley, Agnes Gay, Walter Sanders, and Louis Foster. John Barkley donated his collection to Cleveland's Case-Western Reserve University.

This was the APIC, held together by a few (15-30) active members who did a lot of corresponding and trading with only infrequent personal contact. Not until 1960 were the first steps taken that directly led to the "active, nationally recognized APIC we share today."

Membership in the APIC has escalated to over 3,000 members, more than a 30 percent increase over the last decade. This non-profit organization serves the entire spectrum of political collecting: presidential, local, third party, woman's suffrage and cause-related artifacts. Today, it encompasses over 30 local chapters and clubs across the United States.

The Big Four . . .

Until recently the ultimate rarities among lapel devices that surfaced on the market were pounced upon by a highly affluent group of gentlemen who became known as the "Big Four." An aura of awe and mystery shrouded these deep-pocketed individuals. Actually their names were Morton Rose, of Bethesda, Maryland; Paul Purlin, who in the late '80s donated his largess to the University of Louisville; Merill Berman, a Westchester, New York investor who exhibited his 30-year collection at the Hudson River Museum in Yonkers, New York in 1984. The fourth member, Don C. Warner, a Westminster, Maryland automobile agency owner, was known to wheel-and-deal new model cars in exchange for prized buttons. Warner's horde of some 850 resplendent buttons was sold at the first and only live auction of a major political collection, the New England Rare Coins Auction in 1981.

APIC's first president, the late Joe Fuld helped sponsor the creation of the Blaine County Museum in Hailey, Idaho. Fuld donated his own vast 5,000 item collection, which is being preserved under an Idaho Humanities Council Grant.

Another APIC stalwart, the highly visible J. Doyle DeWitt, of Hartford, a CEO of Travelers Insurance, had an indelible impact on the hobby. DeWitt began collecting in the 1920s, accumulated artifacts by the thousands and willed his collection to the University of Hartford in 1972. It was not until the spring of 1989, however, that the university completed a campus-based Museum of American Political Life to house this bounty of Americana.

Over the intervening years, Dr. Edmund Sullivan, who later served as the museum's first director, had amassed another 20,000 items through bartering and private donations. The Political Life Museum today ranks as the finest single repository of American political artifacts in the world.

Former presidents Jimmy Carter and Bill Clinton and presidential candidates Barry Goldwater and George McGovern are avid collectors. So too, was the late publisher of *Forbes*, Malcolm Forbes, whose son, Malcolm Jr., vied with noted Chicago labor lawyer Joe Jacobs for the top selling Cox-Roosevelt jugate at the Warner sale. Edwin Mosler, President the Mosler Safe Company, also a caretaker of one of the premier mechanical bank holdings, amassed an imposing political collection which sold a few years ago.

Times have changed in the hobby. Occasionally, a well-heeled collector might make overtures to top all bids and corner the ultimate rarities. The market, however, once dominated by a privileged few, now boasts a broad, solid base of curators, antiquarians and collectors who gather and preserve these physical relics for posterity. This is clearly reflected in the demonstrable growth and vitality of the hobby.

2

THE BASICS

Finding Your Collecting Groove

"Pinbacks are cultural messages—sometimes simple, occasionally complex and ambiguous, but invariably revealing."—John Brewer

An inescapable truism applied to political campaign buttons or pinbacks (the two terms are used interchangeably) in the hobby is that they reign supreme on the covetability scale. To be sure, there are occasional rumblings over such categories as three-dimensional artifacts, textiles, ceramics, glassware, ephemera. Once you've attended any regional bourse or show, or national APIC show or check out the wealth of political mail auction catalogs available, you're clearly in button heaven. It is estimated that over 90 percent of the political collecting universe is button-obsessed.

Many APIC members opt to zero in on a favorite candidate, often one who hails from their home state or relates to their own realm of experience or profession. Other choices stem from a personal tie-in from the past.

Noted collector Don Warner came across a copy of *Life* magazine in his brother's bedroom featuring a cover photo of Wendell Willkie. Many years later, in an attempt to recapture this fleeting vision, Warner scavenged antique stores and flea markets and found that in addition to campaign-related magazines, Willkie and FDR campaign pins and other trinkets also abounded. The late Joe Fuld, one of the APIC founders, recalled in the *Keynoter* his introduction to the hobby: saving up his pennies as a young lad back in 1896 so he could run down to the local dry goods store and buy fascinating little gold and silver bugs from the McKinley–Bryan race.

We know of any number in the hobby who are converts from the ranks of stamps or coins collectors. Coins and stamps are produced by the government in known quantities, with every variety meticulously cataloged and values easily determined. Once one fills out a given set, the challenge, the thrill of the chase is gone. Unlike coins and stamps, buttons were produced by hundreds of private manufacturers, stationers and jobbers at the bequest of local and national campaign committees.

In the next few pages, you will find a choice of viable collecting categories that exist in quantities to build a collection with 1,000 or more objects. In most instances, you won't have to mortgage your house to afford them.

An often overlooked subcategory is the $7/8$ inch button. Ludwig Mies van der Rohe's aphorism "Less Is More" applies here. These pint-sized buttons, or "mighty mites" as they're often known, occupy far less display space; they're available at prices far more reasonable than their larger variants.

David Frent, a leading mail auctioneer from Oakhurst, New Jersey, attests that in recent years, intense competition has prevailed in the bread-and-butter $50 to $100 range.

One of the most popular ways to specialize is to zero in on a specific candidate. In fact, during panel discussions on market trends at recent APIC National Conventions the audiences asked most about how to increase their chances of snaring these elusive entries.

Ten Ways to Gain Greater Satisfaction in Collecting

1. *Sharpen your visual skills.* Visit as many museums, presidential libraries and private collections as possible and carefully peruse their artifacts. Good places to start are the Smithsonian Institution, in Washington D.C., the Museum of American Political Life and the University of Hartford, plus the twelve presidential libraries. A recent exhibit "Historical New Hampshire/First Stop the New Hampshire Primary" at the New Hampshire Historical Society Museum in Concord, provides fascinating insight into an enduring grass roots tradition.

2. *Do your homework.* Immerse yourself in as many reference guides, auction catalogs, trade publications, and press clippings as possible. Two recently published books by Random House, the first to deal with the two major parties in forty years, make compelling reading: *Grand Old Party* by Lewis L. Gould and *People of the Party* by Jules Witcover. The APIC has complete files of its *Keynoter*, an indispensable political reference source you can access at *info@apic.use.* By learning as much as you possibly can about each presidential candidate, you may come across a real find that might be missing a name, date or other signs of identification. Attribution may come to you in a sudden flash of recognition.

3. *Find your niche. Th*e world of presidential campaign collectibles spans over two centuries and thousands of different objects. The biggest folly committed, especially by beginners, is to plunge in and amass a magpie mix of every item in sight. At an APIC convention show a few years ago, Richard Maxson, a fellow dealer/collector, was approached by a leading corporation executive who wanted to place his order for "one of each for every campaign from Washington to G.W. Bush!" This is a dead-end road to confusion, delusion and collector burnout.

There's an old Yogi Berra quote, "If you don't know where you're going, you'll wind up somewhere else." Actually, the entry level collector would do well to generalize, if for no other reason than the education one receives in so doing. It is always important to sit back occasionally and determine what direction you want your collection to take and what limitations need to be set. As you become more familiar with what's out there and feel more comfortable buying and trading items, you might consider specializing; most assuredly, it can provide the depth and sense of cohesion in building your collection, that a general collection cannot.

Choice William McKinleys from 1896-1900; note Gold Bug mechanical at upper right and McKinley on Bicycle, center. From Robert Fratkin Collection.

4. *Seek out seasoned dealers and advanced collectors.* It pays to ask around at APIC and other gatherings to learn who are the most knowledgeable authorities—whose integrity and judgment are respected. The hobby has grown appreciably in recent years and there are many new faces. Ours is, nevertheless, a tightly knit universe and the word is soon out as to who is reputable and who is not.

5. *Don't be intimidated.* It may help to be aware of the relative ranking among candidates as popularity, demand, and availability of material are factored in to determine prices. The most popular are:

George Washington	Franklin D. Roosevelt
John Adams	Alfred E. Smith
Thomas Jefferson	Harry S. Truman
James Madison	Andrew Jackson
Abraham Lincoln	John F. Kennedy
William Jennings Bryan	Eugene Debs

In recent years, the campaign items of Richard Nixon and Dwight Eisenhower have become increasingly popular. Selecting one of the above candidates, or choosing a different one, affords the collector a sense of purpose in the hunt. It is also important to know that most Taft, Bryan, McKinley, and Kennedy buttons and those of many other candidates can still be obtained for a reasonable price. No collector should be intimidated because of the rarefied prices for a relatively few well-publicized examples. Part of the allure of political memorabilia is that it exists in abundance and infinite variety and one may specialize on many different levels.

Fred Jorgensen, a long-time Santa Rosa, California political items devotee once said, "Most collections are made up primarily of good strong items of considerable appeal, but modestly priced. The 'high tariff' pieces don't even make up one percent of the hobby. To represent it otherwise is misleading and does the hobby a disservice."

6. *Expect the unexpected.* Political buttons can turn up in the most unlikely places. In Hartford, Connecticut not long ago, a previously unknown George Washington Inaugural button literally popped up out of the pavement at a traffic cop's foot a few years back, when a construction crew uncovered an old dumping site. Recently, two different variations of a McKinley/TR "Expansion" multicolor button of the pair preventing Bryan from talking down "Old Glory in the Philippines" showed up at opposite ends of the country.

7. *Take Risks.* Resign yourself to the prospect that sooner or later you will make an error in judgment. Take heart as mistakes often pay for themselves once they remain indelibly etched in your mind. This can only heighten your perception in future transactions and keep you humble.

8. *Don't be investment obsessed.* It's possible to take a middle-of-the-road approach with one eye on aesthetic appeal and therapeutic value and the other on investment potential. Ted Hake, whose three-volume *Encyclopedia of Political Buttons* has been the bellwether of prices, as thirteen experts rate 12,000 items and 1,000,000 computerized evaluations on a periodic basis to reassess value and provide price estimates. Prices have all but tripled within five years.

From 1984 to 1991, the overall increase for buttons in the three books was 180.2 percent, with the most dramatic increases coming from the Golden Age (1896–1916.) This begs the question: Is further appreciation possible and will reasonably priced items remain available? Hake feels that the answer is "yes" to both questions, stating, "For many years presidential items were a well-kept secret; large numbers of buttons were undervalued in relation to their degree of scarcity. The graphic appeal . . . and their historical significance will continue to attract collectors."

9. *Be patient.* Even the Franklin D. Roosevelt dynasty didn't happen overnight. Learn as much as you can, keep your eyes open. If the time comes when the spirit of the chase no longer gives you that familiar adrenaline rush, take a hiatus and "chill" for a while.

10. *Collect what you like.* While it may sound simplistic, it is also essential and a lot more fun that you collect what *you* like and not what is considered trendy. Make sure that the candidate or category you choose encompasses items within your financial grasp and concentrate on the finest. An experienced collector once advised, "It is better to have fewer buttons but to find the best that money can buy. It is better to have one outstanding example than a host of inferior ones."

On the Campaign Trail for Buttons

As of November 2004, the next wave of political buttons will have hit the hobby like a tidal wave, unleashing 2,000 to 3,000 different new collectibles.

Political buttons, upon making their initial appearance in a campaign, have the lifespan of a butterfly, and the motto is get them while you can.

Records from recent years show an election fever buying panic which breaks sharply six months or so after the November election. Interest subsides, as does the price in most instances, for the next several years, until a realistic level is reached. Some of the "hot" McGoverns from 1972 and Carters from 1976 originally sold for five to ten times what they bring today. Direct mail dealer Dave Frent writes that he personally waits until eight or nine months after an election before focusing on what he wants for his collection. "I see a better selection, and my dollar goes further."

It is also axiomatic that no current button, such as certain 1976 Carters, no matter how limited their number, or how our ranks grow in the hobby, can expect to hold value like a Grant ferrotype or a Cox or Davis picture pin.

In 1973, a hitherto unknown McGovern slogan button surfaced "I'm a Teamster for McGovern." Suddenly this item became one of the high rollers on the market, selling for $200 at one point before settling back to a more realistic $25. Such "riches to rags" stories can be put on instant replay many times over as relating to untold other campaigns.

Where to find buttons?

First of all, you do not need the sleuthing services of independent counsel Kenneth Starr to deduce where to seek out arcane examples: Two prime sources beckon, official and unofficial.

Official

These are directly related to the political process: political party and candidates' campaign headquarters, rallies, fund-raisers, special interest groups (e.g. labor unions such as the Teamsters or the Chemical Workers), charity and educational organizations and political activist groups. It is amazing how many collectors never take advantage of these valuable sources.

Each election year, the Federal Election Commission (FEC) issues a list of all candidates who have filed with their office—from the Democrats and GOP to the third parties and independents.

Democratic and GOP National Conventions are the ultimate sources for a wide assortment of political artifacts, as many of the true modern standouts are made specifically for that event. As one observer put it, thousands of politicians, delegates, members of the press, vendors and assorted fringe area crackpots converge on the host city. It's always a blast to read in the APIC *Bandwagon* about fellow APIC members who camp out at the Nationals and engage in the frenzy of buying, selling and swapping. Hotel lobbies near the convention headquarters are an excellent source for buttons tailored specifically for the various delegations. These buttons are very desirable in the hobby and may immediately carry a collector value of $10 to over $100. A 1980 Reagan Montana delegation button bringing $3 to $5 at the convention has since appreciated to as much as $50. Not all delegate buttons skyrocket in price. Marc Sigoloff in *Collecting Political Buttons* writes: "The 1984 buttons from Pennsylvania and Nebraska (not readily available to the public) sold for as high as $100 at the convention. Subsequent sales in the hobby, however, brought much lower prices."

Unofficial

These include antiques shows, flea market and garage sales, mail order dealers, auctions and even button manufacturers themselves. In our experience, the most productive and reliable sources are the regional shows or *bourses* (APIC's term for shows or swap meets) and the National Convention conducted under the auspices of the APIC, a non-profit organization which is the backbone of the hobby. The APIC address is: Member Resources, P.O. Box 5632, Derwood, MD 20855-0632., or: info@apic.us.

Some dealers at flea markets and the smaller generalist shows have such delusions of grandeur that pricing is completely beyond reality; one would think every $2 Willkie button to be as precious as a Roosevelt-Cox jugate. There are also some dealers who may, often unwittingly, offer trays of buttons that are blatant reproductions.

Many of our collecting friends report they've found good button prospects in coin and collectible shops, gun shows and car meets. Car meets especially are a time-proven hunting ground, particularly for the incredible variety of the political license attachments and tire covers that became widely popular beginning in the late 1920s and 1930s.

Estate Sales

Our favorite estate-sale story (mostly due to its happy ending) goes back seven or eight years when we received word from a friend that a couple they knew had stumbled on a sizeable stash of political buttons under the stairwell when they first moved in their home. We made the perfunctory call and were subsequently invited to view a fantastic assortment of button beauties from the early 1900s, though most of them were nested inside one another and were rattling around in a shoe box, a real no-no that drives true collectors to distraction.

We tactfully suggested that the buttons be stored separately, inventoried and photographed for insurance purposes, as they represented a sizeable nest egg and told the couple we'd be prepared to make an offer. The husband especially (a pompous sort), however, was vague as to any intention of selling the collection, giving the old story that perhaps one of their children might like them.

Years passed. We still held slim hopes that perseverance would pay off, and periodically checked with the couple but to no avail. Then one day came the shattering news that the couple had moved out of state, and consigned the precious political stash, along with their redware and period furniture collection to a local auctioneer to be offered at an estate sale. Fortunately, the auctioneer, who knew of our passion for political items, elected to sell the buttons separately and called to ask if we wished to be included, along with a number of other area collectors, to bid on the collection at silent auction. Fortunately, being well acquainted with the items enabled us to "sharpen our pencil" and submit the winning bid. By reluctantly parting with one key item, a splendid TR-Johnson 1912 Bull Moose jugate, we immediately recouped our investment. The exultation of securing our greatest find was transcended only by the satisfaction of obtaining the collection for an outlay far below the price we'd been originally prepared to pay the couple.

Mail Auction and Fixed Price Catalogs

In terms of ultimate rarities as well as offering the widest variety of political items available today, the real action is generated by the mail auction folks. One can traverse the nation many times over, hitting every conceivable flea market and group shop, and never see the quantity and quality of buttons currently available from this coterie of mail-order dealers. The hobby is fortunate to have at least a half dozen reputable mail auction and mail catalog entrepreneurs—most of whom are listed with addresses, phone numbers and e-mail contacts in the back of this guide.

eBay

Many collector friends swear by cyberspace as a medium for both selling and buying. Certainly online marketers such as eBay have produced their share of real finds and done much to introduce new collectors to the hobby and broaden the universe. When it comes to political items of extreme rarity, however, disturbing reports persist from frustrated would-be purchasers that certain buying cartels (of which there are many) whose sole function is to constantly monitor the whole bidding process, have been known to pounce upon said item, shoehorning in a winning bid at precisely the last possible second before the designated closing time. This fate could also befall you in a phone or mail-bid auction, but the competition is not quite as cutthroat.

Other Collectors

It is axiomatic that every collector is also a dealer in some degree or another. One of the bonuses of political items collecting is the fascinating individuals you meet. The importance of keeping a good supply of duplicate buttons in stock comes into play here, as good old-fashioned bartering can lead to splendid additions to your collection. Collectors also tend to stay more in line with reality—with prices still within this galaxy.

The most important reason to collect may not be intrinsic to the political artifacts themselves, but to the friendships made with those whose paths never would have crossed had you not shared a special interest.

Detecting Fakes and Fantasies

Copies or reproductions of political memorabilia have been known to infiltrate the hobby, at least since 1889, the centennial of George Washington's inaugural.

Over 90 percent of all bogus material is confined to political pinbacks. The remaining spurious examples seem limited to certain nineteenth-century glassware, medals, posters and other easily faked categories. Invariably they were of a commemorative nature, with no intention of deception.

The APIC, which applies the appellation *brummagem* (brum'-i-jem) to denote repros and fantasies, has documented over 700 pinback fakes. The term is an archaic form of the English Birmingham, a city notorious as a hotbed for counterfeit groats, or coins in seventeenth-century England. Today, brummagem applies to any cheaply contrived object having a showy quality; a reproduction, not the genuine article. One of the many reasons for joining the APIC is their Brummagem Watch: they've also compiled a comprehensive booklet that not only pictures most of the offending buttons to be wary of, but also carefully details how to spot the discrepancies between the original and bogus.

A *reproduction* is a new item, copying the exact design of the original campaign item long after the election is history.

A *fantasy item* differs in that the design never existed in the first place. Some fantasy items seem to have been issued by certain vendors with time on their hands; e.g. a "Transvestite Bobsledders for Kerry/92." An older fantasy, picturing John Fremont, an entry issued in 1906 to commemorate the GOP's fiftieth anniversary, is collectible in its own right.

Another common violation is a *restrike* or *rerun*—a pinback or medal struck from original dies, subsequent to the date of the original issue. Examples produced since 1900 are universally discredited; earlier medalets (c. early 1850s) justify a qualification and are treated on an individual basis.

A *repin* or *retin* generally applies to celluloids that were partially manufactured at the time of the campaign but required additional assembly or manufacture subsequent to that time, e.g., in searching for old campaign buttons, collectors and dealers on occasion, may come across a supply of old button papers that were never affixed on buttons. Long after the election, some purveyors have been known to mate an old paper with a later metal shell and pass it off as legitimate (of the early period).

Reproductions tend to surface in special sets as advertising premiums in the four-year presidential election cycle when recollection of campaigns past have greater relevance. In the late 1960s and '70s, firms such as a Abbott Laboratories, American Oil, Borax, Exxon, Kleenex and Procter & Gamble promoted special sets of litho pins issued originally as celluloids. Another source of reproduction has been the gift shops in presidential residences and presidential libraries. Two examples include a deceptive Harry Truman picture pinback from the Truman Library which bears no markings other than a tiny manufacturer's logo. A JFK–Johnson jugate is properly marked as "Repro for JFK Library 1979" on the curl. Both cellos and lithos are discussed in more detail in Chapter 3. Some of the known reproduction disclaimers follow:

Lithos

"Abbott" used by Abbott Laboratories; also marked "Repro 1968"

AO-1972 (#'s 1-38)—American Oil Co

"Japan" issued by Sunset House

"Kleenex Tissues 1968; Red Garter"—a San Francisco bar

"Vote For Seagrams 7, It's America's Whiskey" tin tabs

Cellos

"Ace 680 N'WAY NYC" by Ace Novelty

"Art Fair 1967 New York"

"Cracker Barrel" reissue of Kleenex set

"Get On the Westinghouse Band Wagon"

"House of Values"; "Liberty Mint 1972"

Legitimate classics of considerable value are more liable to be thoroughly scrutinized. There is, however, an obvious unscrupulous element known to reproduce less expensive, commonplace buttons for a fast buck: an Adlai Stevenson portrait pin; an FDR "Our President" starred portrait and a number of Alf Landon Sunflower variations have surfaced in lithographed tin. A common practice has been to recycle venetian blind slats to stamp out circular disks as repro material.

How To Spot Repros

1. Most of promotional issues such as the Kleenex sets are actually dated and stamped "Repro" or "Reproduction," although some have been known to be scratched out or overpainted. Look for the telltale signs of touch-up.

2. Repros tend to be larger than the legitimate pinback.

3. Only a handful of solid celluloid buttons are known prior to 1896—a scattered few portray Cleveland, Tilden, Blaine, Hayes and Harrison. A cello set produced by a tobacco company from the early 1900s depicting presidents from Washington to McKinley would automatically eliminate all but McKinley as originals.

4. Repros of pinbacks dating from 1896 through World War I are made of celluloid as opposed to litho tin.

5. Almost all celluloid fakes are acetate-covered. Acetate was developed in the late 1930s and after a crossover period, has been used almost exclusively since 1952. Under an incandescent light, you can determine the difference between the two by tilting the button so the light is reflected off the surface to your eyes. Celluloid has an irregular surface and absorbs light, while acetate is nearly 100 percent light reflective.

6. The reverse of a button also bears telltale signs. Earlier cellos feature the inside metal in its original silver state; on many repros the metal may be white or possibly other colors. If the pin has a back-paper, and it is glued in, it is almost always a fake.

7. Slight variations in printing of colors are known among originals, but when there's a drastic difference in color, as is the case of a pasty brown 1$^1/_2$ inch Adlai Stevenson pinback we know of, it's an automatic tip-off that it's a fake.

8. Washington Inaugural repro lapel devices are usually of silver, lead or white brass; originals were issued in copper, deep yellow brass and pewter. (See Edmund Sullivan's *American Political Badges and Medalets 1789-1892* for discrepancies in size.)

9. As Robert Fratkin and Christopher Hearn point out in a *Keynoter* article *How to Use the Brummagem Project,* "the most important facet of collecting is also the most important facet in recognizing a brummagem—education." To prepare yourself for any curves a faker might throw at you, the best remedy is to become familiar with as many original artifacts as possible; scrutinize them closely as to how they look and how

they're put together. At a certain point, this visual and tactual information assimilates, and your sense of whether any given pinback is "right" or "wrong" becomes almost intuitive.

10. As a final caveat, studiously avoid any dealer or entrepreneur who will not unconditionally guarantee his campaign artifacts as authentic.

The Hobby Protection Act

Political item collectors have protection from unmarked reproduction campaign items thanks to two prominent APIC members and former presidential candidates, Senators Barry Goldwater of Arizona and George McGovern of South Dakota. The two succeeded in drafting P.L. 93–167, the Hobby Protection Act, officially signed in 1973 by Richard Nixon, ironically the final act prior to his resignation. The law calls for imitations of buttons and other objects to be clearly marked "Reproduction," or a similar term, in a prominent place on the item itself.

Grading of Political Buttons

Condition—this inescapable buzzword is to political collecting what location is to real estate. The difference between an item that is virtually mint or pristine and one that may be severely flawed profoundly affects aesthetics, not to mention a depreciation of up to 80 percent in value. Political memorabilia collectors, like their stamp and coin collecting brethren, are absolute sticklers on condition and the ever-present loupe almost becomes part of their physiognomy. Even so they must face the reality that in the case of any item, particularly if it's 100 years or older, they may have to settle for less than perfect. Allowances can be made when the flaw lies outside of the image area. Major condition bugaboos are deep scratches or lines; surface bumps, structural damage; fading, foxing or staining; celluloid flaking, serious oxidation of metal parts, missing parts such as a clasp or back paper and improper centering. Flaws such as centering and foxing are irreversible. Political buttons are graded by a system from A+ to E and closely conform to standards set within American Political Items Collectors guidelines.

1. Grade A (Mint or Pristine) items are not usually described at all. In each case, a judgment was made that the visual impact of the button and its physical con-

dition are of superb quality. No obvious marks or imperfections are visible that would detract from the collector's visual enjoyment of the button, and that no flaws exist, except as noted. A grade runs the gamut from Essentially perfect: A+, Excellent: A, to nearly Excellent: A-.

2. Detractions that would rule out an "A" grade, but not necessarily flaws that are visible on a button's surface. With a range of B+ to B, these items would be regarded as Very Good.

3. The buttons have more serious flaws as noted, but in some cases may be included as achieving the highest bids based on rarity and desirability. These buttons would be considered Good to Near Good, varying from C+ to C-.

4. These items would have to be considered in poor condition for the reasons noted. There are a scant few items in this (or the "C" category) ever offered because of severe flaws and they pass muster only because they represent an extreme rarity and are still collectible.

5. Fails to make the grade in acceptability.

Grading on Tokens Medalets, and Shell Badges

Political tokens and medals are coin-like in nature and are traditionally graded on a scale similar to coins. This criterion could also apply to metallic shell badges and other early political lapel devices. Grading criteria correspond to the American Numismatic Association standards.

Uncirculated—Has no trace of wear but may show a moderate number of contact marks and surface may be spotted or lack some luster.

About Uncirculated—Has traces of light wear on many of the high points. At least half of the mint luster is still present.

Extremely Fine—Design is lightly worn throughout, but all features remain sharp and well defined.

Very Fine—Shows moderate wear on high points of design; all major details clear.

Very Good—Well worn, with main features clear and bold, although rather flat.

Good—Heavily worn, with design visible but faint in area. Many details are flat.

Poor—Numerous defects noted that substantially alter appearance of item.

3
THE EVOLUTION OF BUTTONS

Button Manufacturers and Jobbers
Dawning of the Age of Amanda

The invention of celluloid came in 1868 when John Wesley Hyatt and his brother Isaiah produced the nation's first commercially successful synthetic material in response to a billiard ball manufacturer's $10,000 prize for a substitute for ivory. Some 20 years later in 1896, a Bostonian, Amanda M. Lougee, was granted a patent for a clothing button with a textile surface covered with a thin layer of transparent celluloid.

Amanda M. Lougee, whose name is to celluloid campaign buttons what the American flag is to Betsy Ross, sold her patent rights to Whitehead and Hoag Company of Newark, New Jersey. This was the modern celluloid, A.K.A. cellos—the generic button as we know it today.

Cellos

The cello's mechanics are simple: a printed paper or metal disk, called a *planchet* is inserted under celluloid. An inner metal ring, the *collet,* locks the celluloid and disk, of paper or metal (*amalgam*) into place. The outer edge or rim is known as the *curl*. The manufacturer's name usually appears in a *back-paper* insert in the button's reverse. A bar or pin, a continuous piece of wire with one of its ends bent to form a holding portion, is then secured inside the ring or collet.

As Roger A. Fisher writes in *Tippecanoe and Trinkets Too,* "No other innovation in the history of material culture in American politics ever gained acceptance so rapidly or on such a massive scale." Coupled with the innovation of chromolithography, imaginative designs or image of candidates in myriad colors were possible. For about a penny apiece, a pleasing, eye-catching presentation became a reality, ushering in "The Golden Age" of buttons.

Lithograph buttons

Lithos, as they're best known, first appeared during the Harding-Cox 1920 election. Once perfected, the lithography tin process sounded the death knell to the celluloids, as the design and imagery could be printed in any colors directly on the button's metal surface. Unfortunately, design creativity suffered and the popular multicolors all but disappeared in favor of funereal blacks and later, tedious red, white and blues. Lithos also proved more susceptible to scratching and chipping, especially when handled improperly.

In 1982, manufacturers introduced plastic coating as a solution to the scuffing and scratching of the litho's surface. The new, improved buttons first appeared in the 1984 Reagan-Mondale campaign. While the button's plastic coating assures a smooth, lustrous surface, it too has its drawbacks—in this case, lack of durability. Consequently, surface pitting and gouging are common.

Tabs

Lapel device manufacturers (ever on the lookout for the cheapest possible mass-produced devices) introduced the tab—the simplest, most primal campaign device ever conceived. The earliest tabs, made of paper, appeared in the 1908 Taft-Bryan campaign, and were short-lived. The metal tabs were introduced in 1924 and because of their size limitation, they simply named the candidate. For the LBJ-Goldwater race, a number of imaginative picture versions surfaced. Today, campaign tabs have all disappeared, supplanted by the even cheaper paper decals or stickers.

Button Manufacturers & Jobbers

Several hundred are known. The following list includes the more prominent makers.

The Whitehead & Hoag Co., Newark, NJ, 1892-1959
(W.H. was the first and foremost maker through the first 70 years.)

St. Louis Button Co., 1899-1957

Torsh and Franz, Baltimore, MD, 1909-1959

Bastian Brothers, Rochester, NY, 1895-1993
(bought out Whitehead & Hoag in 1959)

Keystone Badge Co., Reading, PA

Western Badge and Novelty Co., St. Paul, MN

C.J. Bainbridge Badge and Buttons, Syracuse, NY

American Art Works, Cochocton, OH, 1904-1981

All Metal Products Co., Springfield, OH

Baltimore Badge Co., Baltimore MD, 1901-1908

Bainbridge (Chas.) Button & Badge, Syracuse, NY, 1907-1959

Bainbridge (H.C.), Syracuse, NY, 1961-1985

Geraghty & Co., Chicago, IL, 1909-1944

Greenduck Corp., Hernando, MS, 1977-1985

Novelty Supply, Pittsburgh, PA, 1927-1931

Oppenheimer and Shaw, Washington, D.C.

Parisian Novelty Supply Co., Chicago, IL, 1905-1985

St. Louis Button & Mfg., St. Louis MO, 1918-1965

Schwaab, S&S Co., Milwaukee, WI, 1938-1968

Scovill Mfg. Co., Waterbury, CT, 1850-1985

Western Button & Badge, Los Angeles, CA, 1915-1961

Waterbury Button Works, Waterbury, CT, 1944-1985

The most comprehensive listing of button manufacturers and guidelines to identification by back papers is Ted Hake and Russ King's *Price Guide to Collectible Pin-Back Buttons, 1896–1986,* published by Hake's Americana and Collectible Press, P.O. Box 1444, York, PA 17405.

Housing and Showcasing Your Collection

"Finding a home" for your political collection is far more than a mere figure of speech. These orphaned relics from the past assume a highly personal, intrinsic aspect, and how and where the material is stored and displayed is limited solely to one's individual tastes, personality, imagination and design sense or creative flair.

One can take a conservative approach as a compulsive accumulator who "squirrels away" his or her collection in safe deposit boxes, bank vaults and packing crates, unlikely to risk overexposure. The opposite extreme is the collector who transforms his home into a museum or shrine, perhaps going overboard and losing touch with the real world.

There is a middle-of-the-road approach that still allows you to live with and enjoy your collection and bask in its reflected glory.

It is important that certain constraints should be exercised. What must be addressed are the inherent dangers in risking artifacts to excessive handling, dust, humidity and direct sunlight, not to mention the ever-menacing problem of security. Discerning collectors wisely rotate parts of their collection, keeping certain items displayed and others carefully packed away in glass-covered frames called butterfly or Riker mounts, enclosed in Mylar or other archival acid-free sleeves, or stashed in specially designed coin cabinets. With Riker mounts, refrain from lining the bottom of the tray with cotton. In high-humidity conditions, the cotton will absorb moisture that could extensively damage the backs of buttons before any signs appear on the obverse.

Deterioration and rapid fading is particularly prevalent among nineteenth-century pinbacks with UV (ultraviolet rays) as a major culprit. The use of drapes effectively blocks sunlight. Fluorescent lighting is recommended to reduce UV problems, but purists argue that this type of lighting tends to distort colors and tones, making it difficult to distinguish certain variants. Low-wattage incandescent mini-shelf lights, arranged in tandem, offer a compromise and show off buttons in their most favorable light, so to speak.

Catalog houses such as Oriac Design, Hold Everything, and Design Within Reach regularly cater to collectors, offering handsomely designed etageres, shelving and curio display cases. Other viable alternatives include resurrected printer font drawers and dental, mechanic, watchmaker, and jeweler cabinets with stacks of shallow drawers.

Above all, refrain from packing your treasures in newsprint or other makeshift wrapping materials—an open invitation to disaster. Newspaper inks and acids contained in many paper and plastic wrappings take their toll. Here are some environment-friendly storage alternatives:

1. If the storage area is subject to temperature changes or is occasionally damp, a dehumidifier is imperative. In smaller enclosures, collectors and dealers frequently rely on crystal desiccants often used by jewelers and tobacconists to reduce moisture content. At the very least, use a relative humidity indicator in the area to monitor changes. Adequate ventilation is also critical.

2. Buttons should be suitably packed to avoid vulnerability to breakage or dinging. Do not overcrowd buttons. Items that are particularly delicate should first be packed in smaller containers. Keep boxes well labeled and key their contents to a computerized or Rolodex listing for quick referral.

3. Set boxes on wooden frames or on castors rather than directly on concrete floors, which may retain moisture.

4. Store all artifacts in darkness; this ordains that each box or other container should have a cover. This precaution is essential for buttons, but applies equally to ephemera and textiles.

5. Place shell badges and any metallic objects in tarnish-resistant bags, which can be usually purchased at your local jeweler.

Inventorying and Insuring Your Collection

Study the whole picture of insuring your collection. Arrange a meeting or two with your insurance agent so that every aspect of the arrangement is clear in your mind. In recent years, homeowners and also renters' policies have become more comprehensive in coverage.

Ray Haradin, a noted militaria dealer/collector writes, "The dichotomy of insurance is, if you fully insure your collection the premiums you pay generally offset the appreciation of you collection. I still recommend insurance and in many instances your collection will be covered under the contents portion of your homeowners insurance.

Although rates vary, the insurance industry generally assumes that collectibles appreciate at five percent a year. They will compare this value, based on your receipts, with the appraised value. Should there be a large discrepancy between adjusted purchase price and the appraised value, a professional appraiser should be consulted."

Another option is to purchase a fine arts rider (also called a floater or endorsement) to a standard homeowner's policy. This rider can insure selected artifacts at predetermined values. It's well worth the added outlay, as your artifacts can be insured at true value (which you can increase to adjust to the prevailing market). Further, the rider is not subject to deductible or depreciation allowances, as often happens with homeowners' policies. Fine arts riders can usually be negotiated; provisions are not so restricted as in regular policies.

Maintain an up-to-date inventory, a written record (insurance companies love receipts) of what you paid for items, backed up by a photographic record of each item. This is imperative. We know many collectors who have purchased video cameras and methodically documented each and every artifact for posterity.

Entry level collectors, especially, should avail themselves of a numbering system that is the standard reference among dealers and collectors. There are several available systems, including one devised by J. Doyle DeWitt in his book, *A Century of Campaign Buttons*. We recommend the Hake system, the most widely-used reference, which has become the standard of the hobby. Dealer Ted Hake, who authored the *Encyclopedia of Political Buttons I, II* and *III* uses a simplified number-coded system for over 5,000 buttons ranging from the most common to the exceedingly rare.

WHAT TO COLLECT

4

"ALL FOR THE CAUSE"—PROTEST GROUPS

Anti-war, civil rights, the environment, radical militants, labor movements, and other impassioned causes represent a highly intriguing, powerfully graphic array of highly collectible "cause" items.

Edmund Sullivan in *Collecting Political Americana*, at one time estimated that "over four thousand buttons had been issued since the early 1960s alone."

Robert Fratkin, in "Political Souvenirs" from the *Time-Life Encyclopedia of Collectibles,* classifies as the most desirable those from the early days of the civil rights movement and those from the mid-'60s protesting the United States involvement in the Vietnam War.

Temperance

Prohibition material, as well as the Suffrage items, have rapidly escalated in price. Most contemporary "cause" material can be purchased at a modest outlay. This plus a certain nostalgic appeal and vibrant colors clearly outclass much of the more recent humdrum material generated by major political parties. Bidding activity on eBay reflects that "cause" material has attracted a new wave of young people to the hobby.

The following comprise specific protest groups that are well worth your attention.

THE WOBBLIES

Few of our history textbooks mention the eternal struggle of unskilled workers for union recognition—workers who often found themselves rejected by and sometimes allied with the American Federation of Labor (AFL).

Many of these workers came from the lumbering and mining regions in the north central and western states and the northeastern textile mills. The ethnic names of many Wobblies and their pacifist leanings aroused rampant xenophobia among the authorities.

Championing their cause, the Industrial Workers of the World (IWW) whose members glorified in being called "workstiffs" and "bindlebums," are more familiarly known as the "Wobblies." Their official anthem was "Solidarity Forever," but possibly more trippingly on the tongue was a tune, actually written by a Wobblie, "Hallelujah, I'm a Bum."

Because public officials felt that many of the Wobblies' beliefs smacked of Communism and anarchy, they were constantly harassed and often incarcerated throughout their stormy history. Since much of the literature and many pinbacks were seized and later destroyed by the U.S. Department of Justice, locating Wobblie material poses a real challenge. Some of the prized Wobblie pins include:

Big Bill Haywood

Haywood, a brilliant Wobblie leader from 1908 to about 1920, inspired several significant portrait pins.

Joe Hill

Though his real name was Haggstrom, Hill was a Swedish-born folk singer in the tradition of Woody Guthrie and Pete Seeger and is known by collectors as the "Troubadour of the Discontented," for his numerous protest songs. He was executed by a Utah penitentiary firing squad.

Arturo Giovannitti and Joseph Ettor

These fiery leaders in the famous Lawrence, Massachusetts Textile Strike of 1912 were pictured "duded-up" in wide brim hats on a pair of coveted pinbacks bearing mottos "A Martyr To the Cause," and " Their Only Crime is Loyalty to the Working Class." Another pin depicts an unidentified Wobblie behind bars inscribed "We're In For You/You're Out For Us."

IWW strikes that inspired pinbacks occurred in Paterson, New Jersey, different locations in Oregon and Washington state and the Mesabi iron ore mining strike in northern Minnesota. The latter yielded pins showing three men behind bars and "Labor" holding the key to freedom; another reads, "Don't Let the Steel Trust Incarcerate These Men for Life."

Sacco and Vanzetti

The saga of Nicola Sacco and Bartolemeo Vanzetti, attracting worldwide attention, ranks as one of the most controversial in labor history. The two Italian immigrants were electrocuted in 1927 for allegedly killing a shoe-factory paymaster and guard and stealing a $16,000 payroll in Massachusetts. Flimsy evidence in the trial led to doubt of their guilt and triggered numerous appeals and worldwide protests. Many observers felt the pair were victims of whipped-up anti-Communist hysteria. One lithograph pin reads, "Life and Freedom for Sacco and Vanzetti" another in red, white, and blue is inscribed, "Remember Labor's Martyrs/Sacco and Vanzetti."

Coxey's Army

Jacob Coxey, a retired army general, led an army of unemployed farmers in a march on Washington, D.C. in March 1894, setting a mass-marching precedent that has been frequently reprised by peaceniks and civil rights advocates over the years. Coxey and his minions, who called themselves "commonwealers," were attacked and jailed by police for trespassing on the White House lawn. The term "Coxey's Army" has become part of our lexicon. A favorite pinback, with a paper insert photo of Coxey, reads "Keep Off the Grass."

United Farm Workers

Often overlooked in the involvement of Hispanics in state and national politics is César Chavez and the United Farm Workers (UFW). Some of the great battles in California's Imperial Valley were pitched in accord with the previously mentioned IWW. Chavez's crusade to improve working conditions for migrant workers is stirringly reflected in relatively easy to obtain posters and pinbacks.

1960s Student Protests and the Anti-War Movement

The Kent State demonstrations, the Columbia University student takeover, and the militant uprisings at the University of California at Berkeley all come back into focus with at least several hundred "flower power" and peacenik pop art and psychedelic buttons issued between 1963 and 1972. Plenty of crossover interest finds stimulus in the failed presidential campaigns of Eugene McCarthy and George McGovern. Pinbacks with graphics and mottos resonating against the Vietnam War, excessive nuclear testing, the drug culture and environmental concerns constitute by far the cleverest, most imaginatively-conceived buttons in modern times and fortunately, are still underpriced.

Women's Suffrage

In 1777 Abigail Adams, writing to her husband John Adams, then a delegate to the Continental Congress, threw down the gauntlet, "If particular care is not paid to the ladies, we are determined to foment a rebellion, and will not hold ourselves bound by any laws in which we have no voice or representation."

Although a woman's right to vote was denied for another 143 years, the distaff side would be wooed in subsequent elections with every manner of knickknack or curio from sewing boxes, darning eggs, patch boxes for cosmetics, to delicate fans, chintzes and fine chinaware.

1920s Woman's Suffrage pin multicolor; ⅞ in.; Susan Anthony NOW Conference, 1970.

ERA and NOW buttons from the 1960s.

It was not until 1848 that the first Women's Rights Convention was organized in Seneca Falls, New York, under the leadership of Elizabeth Cady Stanton and Lucretia Mott. A month later a second suffrage meeting was staged in Rochester by Quaker school mistress, Susan B. Anthony, the first attempt to organize on a national scale. Later in 1851, Anthony and Stanton merged the two groups to form the American Women's Suffrage Association.

From 1870 to 1910, in almost 500 campaigns on state levels, the Suffs (as they were fondly called by the headline writers of the day), attempted to submit the issue to the voter. Only 17 resulted in referendums—Rhode Island in 1887 and New Hampshire in 1902, among them. Only in Idaho and Colorado were these tactics successful. Colorful flyers and pinbacks and posters used the flag with a star and coat of arms for each of the United Equal Suffrage states. Two other additions came even prior to admissions to statehood—the first being Wyoming in 1869 and Utah in 1896.

Pamphlets and pinbacks urged that women either be exempt from taxation or granted the right of equal suffrage. "What is sauce for the gander is sauce for the goose."

A preponderance of women's rights or Suff collectibles was inspired from 1910 to 1920, a decade known for dramatic parades, hunger strikes, demonstrations, mass arrests and other indignities inflicted on a new militant spin-off sect headed by Lucy Burns and Alice Paul. This faction took a direct confrontation strategy first successfully advanced by British feminist, Emmeline Pankhurst.

A tiny figural ceramic mug in Pankhurst's image bears the rather racy battle cry, "Down with the Trousers." A colorful cartoon postcard of the period pictures a group of Hens with the admonition, "No Votes. No Eggs!"

The Burns–Paul Suffs chained themselves to the White House fence and waved pennants and banners in the faces of congressmen. Buttons featuring Susan B. Anthony, Elizabeth Cady Stanton, Alice Paul, Lucretia Mott, Lucy Burns, Lucy Stone and Stone's daughter Alice Stone Blackwell are highly coveted. Elizabeth Cady Stanton's daughter Harriet Stanton Blatch, of the women's National Political Union was one of the first to issue colorful, stirring buttons. Another mover and shaker, Emily Bloomer, a spirited editor of the tabloid *The Lily*, inspired a new fad—full-length skirts and outlandish pantaloons. Henceforth, in the public mind, Suffragettes became known as bloomers.

Die-cut tin bluebird window-hanger from a Massachusetts Suffrage Chapter. Makes a fitting centerpiece among an arresting array of ribbons and buttons.

Another early leader, Sarah Bagley, the first woman trade unionist of note, organized her "Lowell Girls" in the textile mills of that Massachusetts city in 1845. Especially prized is a metal souvenir thread holder, "Sarah's Suffrage Victory Campaign Fund/Help Cut the Fetters," commemorating that watershed event.

Intense opposition to the women's cause stemmed from a number of special interest groups. In the South, the focus of anti-suffrage lay in fear of the black vote and angst over attempts to overthrow Jim Crow restrictions such as the poll tax. Since many women lent their support to the Woman's Christian Temperance Union (WCTU), led by Francis Willard, Cary Nation and her saloon busters; the Midwest opposition came from the brewing interests; in the East, from business and industrial blocs.

Memorabilia from the "anti" camp cuts across many ideologies and prejudices and appeals to crossover collectors of abolition, temperance, labor, and even Ku Klux Klan items.

A fascinating array of mementos focuses on black activist Sojourner Truth, a former slave who electrified a Suff crowd in Akron, Ohio, with "Ain't I a Woman?" with oratory concluding, "If my cup won't hold a pint and yours holds a quart, wouldn't you be mean not to let me have my half measure full?"

Any items are highly collectible that relate to prominent abolitionist Frederick Douglass who ran as vice-president of the Equal Rights party under Victoria Woodhall in 1872. Other highly collectible items relate to a scattered few black congressmen during the Reconstruction period.

In California, women were granted the right to vote in 1911. At the Pan-Pacific Expo in 1915, a 90-foot high Suffrage statue towered over the pavilions on San Francisco's Treasure Island and inspired miniature souvenirs that were peddled on the Midway. Expos yielded a glittering array of art nouveau pinbacks, ribbons, pennants and other suffrage-inspired treasures.

World War I brought women out of the home and into new spheres of activity. Many would assume men's jobs in industry and public service and serving on the front lines as nurses; this posed a new moral argument reflected in a large poster depicting a suffragette flanked by a World War I military office and enlisted man. The accompanying motto read, "We Give Our Work/Our Men/Our Lives—If Need Be/Will You Give Us Your Vote?"

One can only guess as to which of the convergent influences turned the tide, for in 1920 President Woodrow Wilson and Congress enacted the climactic passage of the 19th Amendment.

Politicians were quick to take advantage of wooing the women's vote. A small red, white and blue pinback from the Harding forces announces "My First Vote is for Harding." Another sought-after pin, a 1³/₄ inch cloth covered beauty states, "Under the 19th Amendment I Cast My First Vote Nov. 2nd 1920"; a ribbon hanger supports the GOP Harding–Coolidge ticket.

Women quickly availed themselves of their newly-won right, helping to boost the vote total from the 1920 election to 26 million, up from the 18 million recorded in 1916.

Contemporary curios issued in the 1960s by militant women libbers such as Witch, Coyote, Red Stockings and the broader-based NOW (National Organization of Women) and ERA (Equal Rights Amendment) espousing everything from anti-nuclear weapons to pro-life, have incited or rekindled a passion for collecting.

NOW's immediate acceptance among college students and faculty, plus shifts in attitude among members of the League of Women Voters provided a strong base to get an equal rights bill through Congress in 1973. ERA material is a highly underrated pursuit. Well over 300 hundred pinbacks, many with colorful and imaginative designs, have been issued over the years. Most items are available on the market for pocket change. Not so the vintage suffrage material which command prices as lofty as the ideals they extol.

It comes as no surprise that many of the leading Suffragette collecters are women. One of the APIC's founders, Agnes Gay, was once herself an activist from the Rochester, N.Y. area. Roberta Batt, a Portland, Maine psychiatrist and her partner Mary Donaldson are noted Suffrage dealers as well as collectors. Cecilia Harris of St. Louis, wife of "Chick" Harris, another APIC founder, has collected women's rights material for over 30 years. Jeannine Coup, editor of *Political Bandwagon* is another avid suffrage collector.

There is no gender gap in suffrage collecting. Frank Corbeil, a maintenance director for the Farmington, Conn. school system, is so immersed in suffrage material that the Smithsonian has recently cataloged his extensive array of relics.

Black History Memorabilia
The Brownsville Raid
On August 13, 1906 a group of 1st battalion, 25th Infantry (colored) troops were accused of staging a raid of this predominately white Texas border town. Following a ten-minute skirmish, 167 armed members of the regiment, who had been dispatched there for field maneuvers, were charged with shooting up the town, firing into homes and narrowly missing women and children.

Officially, a young bartender was killed and a police lieutenant wounded. The motive given was that the raid was in retaliation for racial slights. Some of the 25ths white officers firmly believed that certain "redneck" residents, anxious to be rid of the black soldiers, might have planted evidence to implicate them. All of the 167 blacks charged signed affidavits, disclaiming any knowledge of the raid.

Lacking any shred of convincing evidence, President Theodore Roosevelt moved quickly. Without a trial or hearing, Roosevelt ordered members of all three companies discharged "without honor." Some of the accused had upwards of 15 years of unblemished service; six had won the Medal of Honor; 13 had been awarded certificates for bravery in Cuba and the Philippines.

The furor would not die. Certain lawmakers, including Democrats seeking to embarrass Roosevelt, joined in the plea to rehear the case. Ohio Congressman "Fire Alarm" Joe Foraker mounted a campaign to clear the soldiers. Roosevelt and Foraker had a bitter confrontation at the Annual Washington Gridiron dinner on July 16, 1907. Red-faced and boiling over at this public scolding, Roosevelt could barely be restrained. A vengeful Roosevelt moved swiftly to break Senator Foraker's political hold on Ohio by directing that all future patronage for the state be channeled through Taft.

Later, Roosevelt relented enough to direct Taft to accept applications for re-enlistment for soldiers who could present a reasonable case for their innocence; only 11 were reinstated.

Years later, after reading *The Brownsville Raid,* written by APIC member John D. Weaver, Congressman Augustus F. Hawkins of California felt compelled to introduce a bill calling on the House to "right this grievous wrong."

In 1972, 66 years after the raid, Secretary of the Army Robert Froehike cleared the regiment's military records and granted honorable discharges to those allegedly involved.

Among a number of stirring political cartoons, a 1906 *New York* Age version, depicts a black soldier being led away as Roosevelt goads him with his "Big Stick." Buttons also chronicle the Brownsville Raid, among them a black, red bust portrait pin with the motto, "Remember Foraker and Brownsville." A "Remember Brownsville" 1¼ inch black and white. pin showing four members of the 25th. Infantry standing at attention and captioned: "Discharged Without Honor," has sold for well beyond $200.

The Scottsboro Boys

One of the great causes of the 1930s, the "Boys," actually nine young blacks, were convicted by an obviously racially-biased Alabama jury of raping two white prostitutes. Their plight quickly became a *cause célèbre* among northern liberals. Although none of the men was executed, all spent time in prison, one for 19 years. International Labor Defense (ILD) a branch of the American Communist Party provided legal and moral support in their defense. Several buttons are known, most of which were issued by the ILD. All Scottsboro material brings rarefied prices, up in the $100 range. The only known picture button depicting all nine men has sold for $400 to $500.

Other Black History Items

Collector interest in early anti-slavery-related materials has reached a fever pitch in recent years. One could anchor a comprehensive collection in itself, based on Staffordshire ceramic mugs, plates, tureens, and an ivory Ostrich painted egg, "Anglo American Abolition Society"—all embodying the black transfer Kneeling Slave theme. A superb figurine of Abolitionist John Brown with two little black girls in tow is highly prized as well as "Little Eva and Uncle Tom" salt and pepper shakers.

Another charismatic leader, Harriet Tubman, served as a Civil War scout, spy and one of the leaders in the Underground Railroad. Tubman posters and pinbacks proclaim, "My train never jumped the track, and I never lost a passenger."

The chief attractions for collectors relate to a handful of black congressmen during the Reconstruction era up to the era of Jim Crow. *Cartes de visites* exist picturing Hiram Revels and B.K. Bruce—both U.S. senators from Mississippi; also the first northern black congressman, Oscar de Priest, in 1928. Other "keepers" are various portrait pinbacks of James Ford, vice-presidential nominee of the American Communist party from 1932 to 1940.

Modern black memorabilia dates predominantly from the early 1960s as an integral part of the Civil Rights movement. Also of interest are mayoral candidates such as Carl Stokes of Cleveland, Senators Adam Clayton Powell of New York, Edward Brooke of Massachusetts and Congressmen Charles Diggs of Michigan. At the national level, Eldridge Cleaver's Black Panther organization and his run for the presidency in 1968 are important. The Peace and Freedom Party issued a number of attractive pinbacks for the 1964 and 1968 campaigns. Colorful buttons mark the Reverend Jesse Jackson's periodic flirtations with the presidency with the Rainbow Coalition.

NAACP (National Association for the Advancement of Colored People) buttons, particularly those relating to anti-lynching and abolishing the poll tax are in great demand. Pinbacks and ephemera distributed during the March on Washington on August 28, 1963 and the March on Selma and any other Martin Luther King Jr.- or Rosa Parks-related material merit inclusion.

Collectors also find rich source material in William E. Dubois of the Pan American Congress and Communist Party (he joined in 1961) mementos; also those of 1920s activist Marcus Garvey, whose Universal Negro Improvement Association advocated resettling blacks in independent African states. In 1925 Garvey was convicted and jailed for fraud and later deported to his native Jamaica.

Let us not overlook militant Angela Davis and her "People Before Profits" pinbacks in her several runs for vice-president on the Communist ticket; also comedian Dick Gregory, known for his hunger strikes, who actually received more votes than Eldridge Cleaver in the 1968 race.

In 1972 New York congresswoman Shirley Chisholm became the first black woman to vie for the highest office. Her buttons were catchy, with the slogans "Take the Chisholm Trail to 1600 Pennsylvania Ave." and "Shirley Chisholm for President to represent *all* Americans";

both rate high with black feminists and hopeful collectors. The latter buttons featured a portrait of Chisolm framed by the female gender symbol.

Other Causes

Other political and cause subcategories that offer a wealth of pinbacks, 3-D and ephemera are as follows:

Native American Militants

Collectors zero in on fascinating material relating to the Battle of Wounded Knee of 1890; General George Armstrong Custer and his 7th Cavalry's Last Stand at Little Big Horn in 1876; the American Indian Movement; the clash with federal forces at Pine Ridge on March 25, 1973 and the ongoing quest by Indian activists to dismiss murder charges against Russell Means, the martyred jailed leader of the American Indian Movement of Colorado.

The Far Far Right
Father Charles Coughlin

Look for material associated with the "Radio Priest" of Golden Oaks, Michigan who regularly engaged in diatribes on the air and in his weekly tabloid *Social Justice*. Coughlin inveighed against Jews, blacks and other minorities in the 1930s, attracting a depressingly dedicated following. A strong political connection exists with Father Coughlin's slander of FDR (Franklin "Rosenfelt") and support of William Lemke, a Liberty party presidential nominee in 1936.

Ku Klux Klan, Copperhead, Know-Nothing Party

Collectibles from these so-called hate groups reflect deep-seated opposition to any progress made by minorities. Outrageous prices are paid today for any of the "hate" material generated by the white-hooded Ku Klux Klan, a secret society stemming from the early years of Reconstruction to champion white supremacy by means of terrorism and intimidation, including cross-burnings and lynchings. The Klan saw a revival in Georgia, Ohio and Indiana in 1915 and exists to this day. Confederate cavalry hero General Nathan B. Forrest was said to be the first Grand Wizard of the Ku Klux Klan, an illiterate misspelling of the Greek word *kuklos*.

Huey Long

The Louisiana Kingfisher, a demagogue, and a passionate anti-New Dealer, was immortalized by a Robert Penn Warren–Pulitzer Prize-winner *All The King's Men,* made into a 1949 movie. He became a cult figure with his grandiose but popular program of public works, the "Share the Wealth" program. Lofty prices are paid for pinbacks picturing Long as a failed presidential hopeful and for his successful run for the U.S. Senate. He served from 1931 until his assassination in 1935.

5

SPECIALTY ITEMS

First Ladies

Many observers regard political pinbacks honoring the first ladies or would-be-first ladies and other members of the first family as one of the most fascinating aspects of our material culture. Superb colorful examples can still be procured for only a few dollars.

Abigail Smith Adams, wife and mother of the second and sixth presidents John Adams and John Quincy Adams; Dorthea "Dolley" Madison, a snuff-taker who rescued priceless paintings and furnishings before the British pillaged and burned the White House in 1814; and Lucy Webb Hayes, "Lemonade Lucy," an ardent Prohibitionist—these passionate partisans were part of a coterie of first ladies who did not hesitate to play major roles in politics and the nation's history.

1960 Pat Nixon; pink, black; 2¼ in.

Frances Folsom Cleveland, a lovely debutante, was the first bride to be married in the White House. Edith Boling Galt Wilson, Woodrow Wilson's second wife, actually acted in her husband's behalf in running the country when President Wilson suffered a stroke late in his second administration. That period of convalescence, which began in early October 1918 and ended in April that following year, was known as "Mrs. Wilson's Regency." Her detractors called it the "Petticoat Government." Ironically, this Southern gentlewoman vigorously opposed woman suffrage. Lou Henry Hoover served as President of the Girl Scouts of America while her husband, Herbert, was in office.

Eleanor Roosevelt was an international figure in her own right, a world traveler, and author of a daily newspaper column, "My Day." Appointed a United Nations delegate by Truman in 1945, Mrs. Roosevelt's Declaration of Human Rights, adopted by the UN, stands as one of the great freedom documents of all time. Of all the first ladies of the modern era, Eleanor Roosevelt came under greatest scrutiny and was cruelly lampooned in a deluge of GOP campaign material (See Willkie; 1940 race).

When Bess Truman, who had outlived all other first ladies, died in 1982, she was accorded a fitting headline tribute in the *New York Times*, "Bess Truman Is Dead at 97; Was President's Full Partner."

There is, of course, the one and only Jacqueline Kennedy, who at the time of JFK's assassination, according to a Gallop Poll, was acclaimed as the most admired woman in the world. The Democrats begged her to seek the vice-presidential nomination but she elected instead to concentrate on building the Kennedy legend. Jackie Kennedy was the driving force in planning the John F. Kennedy Memorial Library in Boston, which opened in 1989.

Actually making candidates' wives a focus of campaign lapel devices goes back to 1856, when the name of Jessie

Benton Fremont was used in a Republican "John C. Fremont For President" race. Jessie's father, Thomas Hart Benton, of Missouri, was well connected and the Benton name was obviously deemed a political asset. A few early inaugural or commemorative examples are also sought after for Francis Cleveland and Edith Wilson. The first first lady, Martha Dandridge Custis Washington, is pictured, along with her husband George, in a number of commemorative lapel devices that were issued during the U.S. Centennial Exposition in Philadelphia in 1876.

It was not until the 1960s, however, when the major parties began to capitalize on featuring first ladies, many of them highly photogenic vote-getters in their own right. A number of pinbacks in the 2-inch to 6-inch size, often in unusual pink and pastel colors, are highly collectible. First lady campaign items undoubtedly influenced the women's vote and played a role in getting their husbands elected.

The following, in alphabetical order, by President's last name, is a sampling of the fascinating variety of first lady material to seek out.

"Our First Couple/Bill and Ernestine Bradley" 2000 hopeful primaries jugate; multicolor; $1^1/_2$ in.

"Bush for President" waist-up photo of George Bush and wife Barbara; multicolor; $1^3/_4$ in.

"Seniors for G.W. Bush 2000" portraits of George W.'s parents, George H.W. and Barbara Bush.

"Laura Bush/A Real First Lady"; multicolor; $1^3/_4$ in.

"Ask Amy" a pinback inspired by Carter's inane and transparently self-serving reference to his daughter as an opponent of nuclear proliferation, during a televised debate.

"I Helped put the Carters in the White House," jugate of Jimmy and Rosalynn Carter.

"Rosalynn (Carter) and Muriel (Mondale) for First Ladies: jugate portraits; r, w, b, blk; $1^1/_4$ in.

"Rosalyn Carter for First Lady in '76"; w, blk; $1^3/_4$ in.

"Jimmie & His Best Friend" jugate portrait of Jimmy and Rosalynn

(Jimmy Carter's mother Lillian graced a senior citizen's button and daughter Amy Carter frisbees were given out at the Democratic convention.)

"Vote for My Daddy/Bill Clinton for President/Chelsea Clinton" controversial pin picturing Chelsea; pin was withdrawn when Hillary objected to her daughter being used for campaigning; multicolor; 2$^1/4$ in.

Hillary R. Clinton heart-shaped stars-and-stripes "no name" pin with oval image of Hillary; r, w, b, blk; 2 in. h.

"Reelect Bill in 1996; Make Hillary President in 2000"; pictures of Bill and Hillary Clinton; w, blk; 2 in.

"Gays and Lesbians for Hillary for U.S. Senate," r, w, b, P; 1$^1/4$ in.

"Hillary/I Want to Be Your Senator" 2000 New York issue; r, w, b, blk; 2$^1/4$ in.

"Hillary and the Seven Dwarfs" portrait of Hillary in center surrounded by other 2004 Democrat hopefuls, Lieberman, Kerry, the Rev. Sharpton, etc., multicolor; 3 in.

Anti–Hillary Clinton

"I Am for Bush & Cheney and Hillary for Ambassador to Arkansas" trigate; multicolor; 1$^3/4$ in.

"Hillary: The broad who would be king" portrait of Hillary Clinton; w, b, blk; 2 in.

"Save Our State of New York/Hillary Clinton Unleashed" cartoon of Hillary Clinton hovering over New York City skyline; multicolor; 3 in.

Dwight & Mamie Eisenhower jugate (no name) with bust portraits; 1952; b,w; 1$^1/4$ in.

"Mamie for First Lady" slogan button 1952; r, tan, blk, 1$^1/4$ in.

"Mamie/Pat" jugate photo pin of Mamie Eisenhower and Pat Nixon; r, w, b; blk; 1$^1/4$ in.

"Mothers for Mamie/Keep a Mother in the White House;" slogan appears inside heart; r, w, b.

"Betty's Husband for President in '76," slogan pin; b, w: 2$^1/2$ oval.

Betty and Gerald Ford no name oval jugate 1976; b, w: 2¹/₄ in. w.

"Betty is Our First Lady" 1976 picture pin; r, w, blk; 1¹/₂ in.

"I'm Betting on Betty's Husband" jugate portraits of Gerald and Betty Ford; bw, b, 2¹/₂ in.

"Keep Betty in the White House" slogan pin; w, blk; 1¹/₄ in.

Jessie Benton Fremont, wife of John Fremont, Republican candidate in 1856; no-name lapel device; b, w; ferrotype in metal frame; 2 in. (A medalet also appears in her image with slogan "Jesse's Choice.")

"Indiana's Favorite Family"; jugate of Barry and Peggy Goldwater; w, blk; 1¹/₄ in.

"Peggy (Goldwater) for First Lady; slogan pin; w, blk; 1¹/₄ in.

"La Primera Dama 2000; Tipper Gore"; Aztec design; multicolor; 6 in.

"Tipper Rocks/Democratic National Convention"; Large print and stars on drum head; r, w, b, blk; 6¹/₂ in. plastic drum pinback.

"Colorado for Gore/ Lieberman"/Sept. 23, 2000/Kristen Gore; portrait of Al Gore's daughter Kristen; multicolor; 2¹/₄ in.

Herbert and Lou Henry Hoover, pair of no-name matching celluloid covered portrait clothing buttons; multicolor; 1¹/₂ in.

"Muriel for First Lady" portrait Muriel Humphrey, r, w, blk; 1¹/₄ in.

"We Love Muriel" portrait Muriel Humphrey; r, b, blk; 1¹/₄ in.

"PAT/For First Lady" 1960 portrait pin; w,b; 1¹/₄ in.

"A Winning Team/Pat & Dick Nixon," 1960 jugate; r, w, blk: 1¹/₄ in.

"We Want Pat Too" 1960 Pat Nixon bust photo; r, w, b, blk: ⁷/₈ in.

"Thelma (Pat) for First Lady" portrait pin (Thelma being Pat's actual first name); w, b; 1¹/₂ in.

Anti-Johnson

"Keep America Beautiful/Get Rid of the Birds (Luci, Lady, Linda);" black script on Y; 1³/4 in.

"Lady Bird Start Flying/Barry Is Coming" slogan pin; r, cr, b; 2¹/4 in.

"We Don't Want Lady Bird Either," slogan pin; r, w, b; 3 in.

"Welcome Ladybird/Flying Whistlestop," cartoon pin of Ladybird Johnson in open cockpit of a bi-plane; b, w, 1¹/4 in.

"America's First Lady" Jackie Kennedy portrait pin; r, w, b, blk' with tinted portrait; 3¹/2 in.

"Remember When America Had a Real First Lady?" pictures Jackie Kennedy in evening gown with Lyndon Johnson in background; w, blk: 2 in.

"Woonsocket's Own"; picture profile of Mrs. McGovern born in that Rhode Island city; w, blk 1¹/4 in.

William and Ida McKinley, 1901 no-name jugate McKinley memorial issue with vignette of McKinley homestead sepiatone; 3¹/2 in.

"President and Mrs. Wm. McKinley" jugate portraits; b, w, blk, ⁷/8 in.

Ron and Nancy Reagan; no-name, waist-high photo of couple wearing sheepskin jackets; multicolor; 2⁷/8 in.

"Nancy Reagan for First Lady;" bust picture of smiling Nancy Reagan; b, w, blk: 1³/4 in.

Ronald and Nancy Reagan; no name image of first couple riding in open limousine; multicolor; 2 in.

"Welcome to Iowa/Aug. 5, 1982" Nancy Reagan single picture pin; b, w, blk; 2¹/4 in.

"For First Lady/Edith Willkie" bust portrait versions in b, w; 1¹/4 in, (also and in reddish bn; and one gold, w.)

"Eleanor Power/California Demo. Women" bust portrait of Mrs. Roosevelt from 1972 McGovern campaign; r, w, blk; 1¹/4 in.

Eleanor and Franklin D. Roosevelt pair of no-name matching clothing buttons; multicolor; 1¹/2 in.

"White–Wayne–Edwards Counties/Welcome Mrs. Roosevelt, June 15, 1936; Illinois whistle stop for Eleanor" r, w, b, blk with ribbon; 11/4 in.

Anti–Eleanor Roosevelt

"Eleanor? No Soap" anti-Eleanor R.; b, w; 1⁵/₈ in.

"Eleanor, Start Packing/the Willkies Are Coming"; b, w; 1⁵/₈ in.

"We Want Edith Not Eleanor" slogan pin; navy b, bk, p, 1¹/₂ in.

"I Don't Want Eleanor Either," anti-FDR slogan pin; b, w; 1⁵/₈ in.

"My Day/When I Vote for Willkie" snide reference to Eleanor's syndicated national column by that name: b,w; 1⁵/₈.

"Project #UMP-000/Sponsored by Eleanor" (anti-FDR issued by Willkieites) cartoon of outhouse; b, w.; 1⁵/₈ in.

Pair of picture pins; Willkie and wife Edith; smiling Edith wears stylish hat; w, blk; 4 in.

"Roosevelt is buying the Aquacade to keep Eleanor Ho(l)me;" (1940 anti-FDR, takeoff on Billy Rose's N.Y, World's Fair event starring famed swimming beauty; alludes to Eleanor's many trips out of the country; b, w; 1⁵/₈ in.

"Washington Sweepstakes/1st Wendell, 2nd, Franklin, 3rd, Eleanor; " 1940 b, w, slogan pin, 1⁵/₈ in.

"Rather an Hour With Edith than 'A Day' With Eleanor"; another anti, touting Wendell Willkie's wife Edith; b, w; 1⁵/₈.

Allice Longworth Roosevelt (Theodore Roosevelt's irrepressible daughter) appeared on a 1¹/₄ in. sepia button.

"President Wilson and His Charming Wife" ribbon with suspended button; Wilson in top hat with wife Edith; three quarter views; silver lettering on off-white ribbon; br, w; 3¹/₄ in.

Woodrow and Edith Wilson, c. 1918 jugate sepiatone in brass-rimmed frame; 3 in.

White House Pets

Even animal lovers have their own political collecting niche as White House pets have had their own 15 minutes of fame; FDR bristled when the GOP charged that he'd wasted a lot of taxpayer's money on travel for his pet Scottie, Fala. "These Republican leaders have not been content with attacks—on me, my wife, or my sons, No . . . they include my little dog Fala . . . I have the right to resent, to object to libelous statements about my dog." A number of pinbacks picture "Checkers," the Nixons' Cocker Spaniel that inspired RMN's impassioned TV "Checkers Speech" in the 1952 race. Animal lovers in 1964 were furious when Lyndon Johnson's photo was splashed in newspapers across the nation as he playfully held up a pair of his Beagle pups by their ears.

"Cat Lovers for Bush In 2000" pair of kittens; multicolor; 2^1/$_2$ in.

"Fala" Me To the Polls"; lapel pin; die-cut image of FDR's faithful Scottie, Fala: ^{1}/$_2$" wood, tin, cloth.

"Laddie Boy" Warren Harding's wirehaired terrier appeared in die-cut pins and even memorialized in bronze statuette in 1920 race.

"Socks"; The Clintons' first pet, a black-and-white feline appears on pin "Like (Socks rebus) Socks Rodham Clinton"; w, blk; 2 in.

"Socks Fan Club"; with cat's footprint reversed out of black; 2 in.

"The Only Clinton I like is (Socks picture) Socks Rodham Clinton;" w, blk; 2 in.

Female Candidates

Many observers have long labored under the misconception that political memorabilia collecting is a male-dominated pursuit. While this may have been true back in the dark ages before suffrage and the women's movement, we know of countless passionate distaff political item collectors, many of whom share the fascination of campaign relics with their husbands or forge in new directions on their own. Any number of female politicians have made an impact in the national political arena. Victoria Claflin Woodhull, a flamboyant lawyer and newspa-

per publisher, leads the parade of feminists who have actively aspired to the presidency. An 1870s cartoon by Thomas Nast, shows her with horns and clawed devils wings, and clutching a "Free Love" broadside. In 1872, Victoria Woodhull with Abolitionist Frederick Douglass as a running mate, became the first woman to run for highest office under the Equal Rights a.k.a. Cosmo–Political Party banner. The voting count results proved too meager to be recorded.

Belva Ann Lockwood was a teacher, suffragist, lawyer and ardent advocate of world peace. The first woman to argue before the U.S. Supreme Court, her biggest claims to fame were drafting suffrage amendments and framing the law that entitled women to have equal rights with men in the District of Columbia. Lockwood founded the National Equal Rights Party in 1884 and vied for the top spot with running mate Marietta Snowman in 1884 and 1888.

Some 75 years later, in 1964, U.S. Senator Margaret Chase Smith of Maine was placed in nomination at the national GOP convention as a first-time woman presidential candidate from a major party. Prized mementos of the occasion include a highly desirable multicolor 3-inch oval button pictured above; also a red, white, and blue portrait pin, "For President/Margaret Chase Smith."

In 1972, New York congresswoman Shirley Chisholm became the first black female candidate for president as one of many challengers in the New Hampshire primary that included George Wallace, Eugene McCarthy, Edmund Muskie, and former New York City mayor John Lindsay, among others. Other female presidential hopefuls through the years included Ellen McCormack, an

Maine Senator Margaret Chase Smith marked her bid for the presidency in 1964 with this multi-colored oval pin.

New York Congress-woman Shirley Chisholm, a 1972 presidential hopeful; black, white; 1¼ in.

anti-abortion advocate in 1976 and Pat Schroeder of Colorado in 1988.

In 1984, New York congresswoman Geraldine Ferraro made history when Democratic presidential nominee Walter Mondale invited her to join his ticket. For a selection of choice Mondale–Ferraro buttons, see 50th Election—1984.

A few distaff candidates for lower office pins have recently escalated in value: a Garry Trudeau "Doonesbury" cartoon pin pictures "Virginia Slade For Congress;" also a "Marilyn Seals For Governor 1970/Peace Freedom" California issue. Also piquing interest is Maryland's Katherine Kennedy Townsend (daughter of Bobby Kennedy) senatorial pin for 2002 and several "Free Angela" (Angela Davis) Communist Party pins.

As more and more women assume pivotal roles in the political arena—for example, Senators Hillary Rodham Clinton; Elizabeth Dole; Barbara Boxer; former Texas Governor Ann Richards; former New Jersey Governor and EPA Administrator Christine Todd Whitman; former Illinois Senator and 2004 Democratic hopeful Carol Moseley Braun; and Condoleezza Rice, George W. Bush's national security adviser—we'll see a groundswell among women who'll join us as equal partners in this captivating collecting venture.

Party Animals

A significant whimsical pinback collection could be assembled focusing solely on party animals, those endearing symbols that have come through the years to symbolize a specific political party or splinter group.

The person who played a major role in the evolution of the Democrat donkey and the Republican elephant, the Tammany Hall Tiger and even Uncle Sam and Santa Claus as we know them today, was Thomas Nast, whose often vitriolic political cartoons graced the pages of *Harper's Weekly* from 1859 to 1886. So strong was Nast's influence that every candidate he endorsed won. His repeated attacks on William Marcy "Boss" Tweed, the corrupt Tammany leader, contributed to Tweed's imprisonment in 1871. Partly due to his unflattering depictions of candidates Horace Greeley and Samuel J. Tilden, their careers were all but destroyed.

The elephant first came to represent the massive GOP vote in an 1874 *Harper's Weekly* cartoon, "The Third Term Panic," in which Nast showed a pachyderm is about to plunge in an abyss marked "Chaos," a trap set by *The New York Herald*. Oddly enough, the Democratic Party was portrayed as the fox in this cartoon; the donkey or ass masquerades in a lion's skin (a reference to one of Aesop fables) represents U.S. Grant's intention of running for a third term.

Although the donkey has been an enduring Democratic symbol since 1875 or 1876, the rooster has appeared in that role on any number of occasions, most notably in the campaigns of Winfield Scott Hancock in 1880; William Jennings Bryan's three races beginning in 1896 and Alton Parker in 1904. The camel served as the symbol for the Prohibition Party later in the nineteenth century. In the early 1900s, a billy goat represented the Populist Party and a goose, the Suffragettes. A raccoon symbol was associated with Henry Clay in his three races in 1824, 1832 and 1844 and he earned the moniker "The Same Old Coon," which appears on a number of ribbons and trinkets. Clay's coon contrasted with rival Martin Van Buren's little red fox symbolism.

Another influential cartoonist, creator of the teddy bear, Clifford K. Berryman, joined the *Washington Post* in 1896 but left two years later and spent the rest of his career with the *Washington Evening Star*.

The story is well documented as to the cartoon of Berryman's "Drawing the Line in Mississippi" in 1892 and how it inspired the Theodore Roosevelt teddy bear. It shows Roosevelt standing with his back to a defenseless, tethered bear cub, which he adamantly refuses to shoot, raising a hand to stay the execution. In a well-documented account, Roosevelt had been unsuccessful in sighting, much less bagging a bear in a two-day hunt and his embarrassed hosts dragged out a scraggly toothless old bear, not a cuddly cub.

Ideal Novelty Toy Makers came out with the lovable plush stuffed creatures in 1903, and Steiff soon fol-

lowed—the rest is history. From the famous Roosevelt Bear Hunt cartoon on up through the Truman years, Berryman would include a little teddy, often bearing little pithy comments, in every presidential cartoon he drew.

Oddly enough, while the teddy bear was incarnated in all types of 3-D campaign material from toys and banks to puzzles, the little creature's image rarely appears on pinbacks. A notable exception is the 1905 inaugural 1³/4-inch black-and-white cartoon pin, "Four More Years With Theodore," showing Roosevelt–Fairbanks in top hat and tails and a flag-waving teddy high-stepping parade style to the inaugural ball. A few charming stickpins, embossed clothing buttons and a "Teddy's" brass match safe are known. Actually, Roosevelt was never all that enamored of the little creature, and

Celluloid sepia-tone buttons featuring William Jennings Bryan and Theodore Roosevelt-Charles Fairbanks affixed to cast-iron party animals.

Teddy Bear Bread Advertising button, early 1900s; multicolor; 1³/₄ in.

was even less thrilled over his new nickname, "Teddy."

Berryman was the creator of another politically-derived animal symbol, the Billy Possum associated with Roosevelt's successor, William Howard Taft. The symbol reportedly was inspired when, as president-elect, Taft ordered his favorite "possum and taters" as a main course at a charity banquet. The possum symbol figures in a wide variety of Billy Possum pins, as well as stuffed animals, figural silver spoons, still banks and even a "Happy Billy Possum's Prosperity Puzzle." The skill marble game's illustration shows Teddy with his bags packed ready to vacate the White House as Billy Possum struts into view.

Billy Possum never achieved the celebrity status of the Teddy Bear. One theory is that the possum image was bit of a "stretch" for the 300-pound Taft. A pundit unkindly quipped that a walrus might be more appropriate.

Theodore Roosevelt was the progenitor of yet another party symbol, the Progressive Party's Bull Moose in the 1912 campaign. When Roosevelt bolted the Republican Party, he tossed his hat into the ring with the third party exulting, "I feel as strong as a Bull Moose." The name became synonymous with the Progressives, and the large antlered creature adorned campaign pennants, bandannas, and scores of colorful buttons and tabs.

1988 New York Congressman Jack Kemp (helmet refers to his being a former NFL quarterback); 1964 Barry Goldwater; 1956 Dwight Eisenhower gilt lapel studs.

For trivia fans, Theodore Roosevelt is the only president to have an actual species of animal named in his honor—the Roosevelt Elk that still roams the Pacific Northwest.

Advertising-Related

When collectors think of political artifacts relating to advertising, they most likely hark back to those colorful, whimsical chromolithograph advertising trade cards that were so popular from the 1880s to the early 1900s. They would do themselves an injustice not to take a good look at bold and brazen buttons hailing from this same era. Buttons, like miniature billboards, resonate as a highly viable area of specialty all its own.

It may come as a surprise that certain objects of your heart's desire, several of which rate among the top ten classics, were inspired not by a political party but by enterprising merchants wishing to capitalize on a presidential election or other memorable historic occasion.

These wily advertisers, one step removed from snake oil peddlers, often invoked the dignity and prestige of the highest office in the land. Unwittingly, presidents became pitchmen whose endorsements were gospel as their names and prestige helped peddle products. They promoted everything from cigars to hair restorers, brain tonic, milk biscuits and rye whiskey.

At the dawn of the twentieth century, two of the "knockout" cartoon buttons were the "My Hobby/A Winner"

1900
advertising
classic pairing
Theodore
Roosevelt with
Zig Zag, a
popular candy;
multicolor;
1¼ in.

duo of William McKinley and William Jennings Bryan astride hobby horses. Some observers feel that these vibrant 2 inch pinbacks were possibly awarded as a premium.*

Although 1910 was not a presidential campaign year, Theodore Roosevelt's triumphant return to America in June after taking a political hiatus to go on an African safari, in reality, kicked off Roosevelt's run to unseat Taft and regain the presidency two years later. The Goerke Company, a now long defunct Detroit dry goods firm, issued a magnificent button set to celebrate Roosevelt's return. The "killer" piece often called the TR Sunrise "Welcome" pin depicts a large head of Roosevelt superimposed over a bright orange sun with a large city in the background and Uncle Sam doffing his hat to his favorite son. Another entry, often called "TR & the Ark" shows TR in safari mufti, surrounded by a boatload of wild animals. A third button shows Roosevelt, just off the boat at New York Harbor, being hugged by a joyous Uncle Sam. A fourth rather surreal "Teddy Our Lion" pin shows a large male lion with huge mane bearing Roosevelt's face. Examples from this set can also be found without the Goerke imprint.

The following significant advertising gems also are well worth pursuing:

An unusual, seldom seen w, blk pinback promotes "President Viewing New Court House/Compliments 'Lazarus Bros' the Busy Store" shows President McKinley with top hat and cane observing an elaborate-looking edifice under construction.

*Kit Barry, a Brattleboro, Vermont, ephemera dealer, states that the "My Hobby" theme originated with a printing jobber who distributed sets of trade cards as stock cards whereby merchants would imprint their own logo and sales message. Other known hobby-horse riders featured on trade cards, but not on a button, included New York politco Roscoe Conkling, Greenback candidate Ben Butler and Garfield assassin Charles J. Guiteau.

"Rochester for McKinley"; "Commercial Travelers" Initials "C.T." on suitcase; br, cr; $1^1/4$ in.

"Count Me for Lucas Paints and a Full Dinner Pail" McKinley rebus button with his portrait and a dinner bucket; w, blk; $1^1/4$ in.; "McKinley Sweeper Cigars" cartoon image of McKinley bust superimposed on broom head; br, w; $7/8$ in.

"Little Pinkie/The Colonel" by Pepsin Gum; caricatures William Jennings Bryan, who was a colonel in the Spanish-American War, carrying sabre; multicolor; $7/8$ in.

"Bacon, Chappell & Co. Dry Goods/Syracuse, N.Y"; Roosevelt portrait; w, blk; $1^1/4$ in.

"Compliments of Pederson Holslag and Co." sepia photo of Roosevelt; b, w; $1^1/4$ in.

"Local Long Distance Telephone" 1904 die-cut Bell paper hanger for Bell Telephone with TR-Fairbanks jugates; w, blk; $1^3/4$ in.

"Two Winners" TR and "Delicious Zig-Zag Confections"; jugate of Roosevelt and box of candy with Miss Liberty and flag; has unusual clicker back; multicolor; $1^1/4$ in.

Roosevelt "Marvel Flour Souvenir/Our President's Visit, 1902": Roosevelt portrait; r, w, blk; $1^1/4$ in.

"Roosevelt-Fairbanks"; rebus cartoon button; Roosevelt standing on Fairbanks Scale: w, blk; $1^1/4$.

"Teddy Bear Bread," multicolor die-cut dancing teddy bear pin; multicolor, 2 in. high.

"Vote for Roosevelt/Use Maple City Soap"; red, white; $1^1/4$ in. (1904 examples are also known for Democrat Alton Parker and Prohibitionist candidate Silas Comfort Swallow.)

A "Little Prize" jugate photos of 1904 candidates Theodore Roosevelt and Alton Parker; "Eastern Telegraph Daily Fungraph/Philadelphia/260 prizes A Week"; a giveaway with different colored deckled-edge layered felt behind pin; served as a pen wiper; w, blk; $1^1/4$ in.

"White Gasoline Engines" jugate pairing Alton Parker with a model of the White engine; r, w, b, blk; $1^3/4$ in.

"Commercial Travelers for Taft"; "I'm Somewhat of a Traveling Man Myself"; Insurance Co. adv.; Taft circular photo on a large suitcase; gold, br, cr; $1^1/4$ in.

"His Master's Voice/The Campaign Button/Are You a Democrat? Are You a Republican?"; RCA Victor advertising takeoff; shows speaker horn with picture of Taft or Bryan depending how the button is turned; w, blk.

"Furriers for FDR"; picture slogan pin issued by small New York merchant trade group; b, w; $1^1/2$ in.

Coattails

The first coattail campaign item may well be a silk ribbon from Andrew Jackson's bid for president in 1828; it links his popularity with that of Pennsylvania congressman Joel Barlow of Sutherland.

Coattails really blossomed in the 1890s with the advent of the cellos and some of the prime examples emerged from the McKinley and Roosevelt campaigns. The most common link is those on the national ticket for lesser offices—Senate, House of Representatives or governor—who, in essence, ride on the frontrunner's coattails. Quite often this combination results in a trigate (three candidates) or on rare occasions, a quadrigate (four or more).

Arguably, the ultimate coattail may be the grammatically incorrect 1941 "Me and Roosevelt for Johnson" jugate of FDR and Lyndon Johnson when Johnson was a relatively unknown senatorial candidate from Texas. Robert Fratkin, a noted collector who authored "Political Souvenirs" in the *Time–Life Encyclopedia of Collectibles*, writes that he was once offered $200 for this jugate, but "had not Johnson later become President, that button would hardly be worth $10." In October 2003, an Al Anderson catalog estimated the coattail at $6,000.

Coattails invariably generate intense collector interest and have particular appeal to those who specialize in buttons related to a specific slate or state. It isn't necessarily *who's* at the top of the ticket or the notoriety of the candidate seeking the lower office—the operative word is scarcity. Since coattails are intended to be distributed over a limited geographic area, they are produced in limited numbers and scarce in the first place. A few sterling examples: At least four different designs are known of the McKinley–Van Sant trigates, with a favorite, "Our Choice" no-name version in black and gold, and the U.S. Capitol dome and Minnesota state capitol domes are both pictured. A multicolor jugate shows Theodore Roosevelt and senatorial candidate Edwin B. Stuart of Pennsylvania with a large furled flag, a highly desirable $^7/_8$ inch pin. A shamrock design sets off a Wilson–Marshall–Foss–Walsh Democratic slate for 1916. Also popular is a 1904 Poker Hand trigate "Republications Must Elect a President and Control Congress" which pictures Theodore Roosevelt, Fairbanks and congressional candidate Henry B. Cassell of Indiana.

Hopefuls

Here's a stumper appropriate for the quiz show *Jeopardy!*. The following individuals have a common bond: Frontiersman Daniel Boone, orator Daniel Webster, Admiral George Dewey, puppet entertainer Howdy Doody, comedian Dick Gregory, publishers Whitlaw Reed, Steve Forbes, and William Randolph Hearst; televangelist Pat Robinson, syndicated columnist and commentator Pat Buchanan, Governor Jerry Brown, General Douglas MacArthur, Alexander Haig, astronaut John Glenn, pro basketball Hall of Famer Bill Bradley, former NFL star Jack Kemp, industrialist Henry Ford, Senators Margaret Chase Smith, Gary Hart, Edmund Muskie, Ted and Bobby Kennedy, Robert Taft, Eugene McCarthy, ambassador Averill Harriman, the Reverend Jesse Jackson, Huey "The Kingfish" Long and Harold Stassen?

The answer is (Harold Stassen being the only dead giveaway) that, one moment in time, they set their sights on the presidency. Some actually stood a chance; others would need a miracle, and one, (Jack Kemp) settled for a vice-president slot. Aside from political buttons heralding their candidacy, these also-rans have been marginalized as historical footnotes. Hope springs eternal, as embodied by Harold Stassen, a Minnesota Republican known as the perennial contender who ran eight times.

Hopeful collecting is not an overcrowded field, but it's nonetheless an intriguing spin-off. Buttons from the candidacies of Henry Ford in 1920 and Huey Long in 1932, for example, often command as high as $200. Buttons from brothers John F., Ted, and Robert Kennedy,

each of whose aspirations were cut short by tragedy, are highly collectible.

An arsenal of some 30 patriotic/political buttons are known for the Douglas MacArthur boomlet. The General was a three-time bridesmaid, although he never formally announced for the presidency, but waited in vain to be drafted as the choice of a deadlocked GOP Convention in 1944, 1948 and 1952. One of the favorites, a rebus no-name button from 1952 pictures MacArthur's military hat, dark glasses and familiar corn cob pipe; another, a picture button reads "Save America with MacArthur."

Several dozen buttons mark the run of "Mr. Republican" Robert Taft of Ohio, including "Vote Taft/Stop Graft," and a 1952 Eisenhower anti-Taft convention entry, "Remember 1912/Win with Ike or Lose with Taft." (Robert Taft was William Howard Taft's son.)

Inaugurals

Inaugural buttons are a relatively recent innovation, as it was not until the Lyndon Johnson administration that they came into major focus as private vendors decided to get into the act.

Such items, though limited in the past, exist for every president from George Washington to George W. Bush, with the late eighteenth-century clothing button inaugurals obviously the most desirable and pricey. Items produced for inaugurals prior to McKinley's 1896 administration also tend to be very scarce.

Many would nominate a handful of imaginative earlier inaugural examples from the elevation to high office of Woodrow Wilson, Herbert Hoover, FDR and Harry Truman. A number of collectors have gravitated to this specialty due to their availability at reasonable prices. Marc

Sigolhoff in *Collecting Political Buttons*, relates that a blizzard forced cancellation of a gala parade during Ronald Reagan's second inaugural and vendors were stuck with a glut of over 20,000 buttons. Inaugurals lack the appeal of actual campaign items but those collecting a specific candidate avidly seek them.

1917 Woodrow and Edith Wilson inaugural button; white, black; 2 in. with silver on white ribbon.

A sampling of inaugurals that rate high with collectors: inauguration of "Harry Truman/Alben W. Barkley," 1949; D.C. Metropolitan Police die-cut embossed silver shield; 3 in. "Inauguration of Harry Truman/President of the United States/January 20, 1949"; Truman portrait; w, blk; 4 in. Shield specimens are also known for the Eisenhower-Nixon and Kennedy-Johnson inaugurals and generally command prices in the $200 range.

William Clinton "The Cure For The Blues" 1993 inaugural; blue, black.

A Jimmy Carter "Welcome To Washington" large multicolor picture 3-inch button showing Jimmy Carter, wife Rosalynn, and four children is one of the only buttons to include the entire clan.

Memorial

Michael Kelley, in the Winter 1996 issue of the *Keynoter*, "A Nation Mourns," writes, "When death comes to a president, its impact rips through the social fabric. Individual Americans see themselves as having a personal relationship with the man in the oval office. The death of a president affects Americans as if it were a death in the family."

As aforementioned, the nation's almost morbid preoccupation with Lincoln items, photographs, and tokens, from locks of his hair to bloodstained clothes, precipitated the entire memorabilia frenzy. Despite this obvious exception, presidential memorial pinbacks have proven to be one of the less desirable and most readily available collecting specialties. Also exempt are memorial items, especially ceramics eulogizing our Founding Fathers, since any item relating to these earliest presidents is almost nonexistent. Especially esteemed, a ribbon marks the simultaneous deaths of John Adams and Thomas Jefferson on July 4, 1826—the fiftieth anniversary of the Declaration of Independence.

A number of our presidents have gained high office though succession—without going through the process of a campaign or election. Nine of our 43 chief executives were vice presidents elevated to the presidency upon death or the resignation of an elected official. Four men succeeded assassinated presidents, one rose to the top due to his president's resignation.

Departed Presidents and Heirs-Apparent
1841—William Henry Harrison
The ninth President died of pneumonia only a few days following his inauguration. He was succeeded by vice president John Tyler. Over a dozen memorial ribbons for Harrison are known, expressing such sentiments as "A Grateful Nation's Mournful Triumph" and "We Mourn Our Nation's Loss."

1850—Zachary Taylor
The twelfth president died unexpectedly of *cholera morbus*, after serving two years in office. He was succeeded by Vice President Millard Fillmore. Taylor, the last of the Whig presidents, is remembered with at least four ribbons: The most elaborate version depicts Lady Liberty leaning on a large chalice bearing a bust profile of General Taylor and his last words, "I am prepared—I have endeavored to do my duty."

1865—Abraham Lincoln
The sixteenth president was assassinated by John Wilkes Booth at Ford's Theater in Washington D.C. shortly after beginning his second term and was succeeded by Vice President Andrew Johnson. The loss of Lincoln as a commander-in-chief during wartime (FDR

also died at such a time) had an indelible impact—particularly on members of the armed forces.

Eminently collectible among the inundation of Lincoln memorial items, is a ribbon "A Nation's Loss" with a 1864 ferrotype pinback attached and a large oval portrait of Lincoln flanked by angels. A number of bearded Lincoln shellback badges were reissued with black enamel around the edge and mounted on black ribbon to serve as a mourning badge. Frequently medalists also adapted earlier issues and added a death date to Lincoln campaign pieces; the practice also applied to candidates James Garfield, Stephen Douglas, Grant and Garfield. A wave of sympathetic *cartes de visites* was issued, including an image of "John Wilkes Booth, the Assassin" with the Devil himself breathing on his neck.

1881—James Garfield

The twentieth president was assassinated by Charles J. Guiteau, a mentally disturbed, disappointed office-seeker, only months after his inaugural. He was succeeded by Vice President Chester A. Arthur, who finished out the term. As with Lincoln and Grant, Garfield's death was also memorialized with a number of glassware mugs and platters, including compotes with funeral drape patterns.

1901—William McKinley

The twenty-fifth president was shot by anarchist Leon Czolgosz while attending the Pan-American Exhibition. Theodore Roosevelt, his vice president, succeeded him and was reelected in 1904. For the first time, a president's death inspired a celluloid button. Most were quite succinct with portraits and the words "In Memoriam" or "In Memory Of." A pair of exceptions: an oversized 4-inch oval sepiatone pin, "Where our President fell/ Sept. 6, 1901," which pictures the Administration Building at the Pan-American Exposition and is eagerly pursued by crossover Exposition collectors; a 3-inch stunning jugate pictures McKinley with his wife, Edith, and a cameo of their homestead in Canton, Ohio.

1923—Warren G. Harding

Three years into his term of office, the twenty-ninth president died of a heart attack in San Francisco while on a

Western swing amid scandals involving Teapot Dome. Vice President Calvin Coolidge was sworn in as his successor. The scandals surrounding Harding's administration precluded a large outpouring of memorial tributes, though several black and white "In Memoriam" portrait buttons are known.

1945—Franklin D. Roosevelt

Less than a year after entering his unprecedented fourth term, the thirty-second president suffered a fatal heart attack in Warm Springs, Georgia. Vice President Harry Truman filled out his term and was reelected in 1948. A stark black with reverse print portrait pin of FDR inscribed "In Memory of F.D. Roosevelt/April 12, 1945" is one of a handful of those eulogizing the wartime president.

1963—John F. Kennedy

The thirty-fifth President was assassinated by Lee Harvey Oswald while riding in a motorcade in Dallas on November 22, 1963. He was succeeded by Vice President Lyndon Johnson. A particularly poignant "Let Us Continue" button with ghosted image of JFK behind a somber Lyndon Johnson is one of the classics marking LBJ's bid for re-election in 1964. Kennedy pinbacks are readily obtained; one of the most appealing is a $3^1/_2$-inch item, "In Memory of Our Beloved President," his portrait, name, and the dates "1917–1963."

1974—Richard M. Nixon

The thirty-seventh president, after releasing transcripts implicating him to Watergate cover-up activities, resigned on August 9, becoming the first president ever to do so. Nixon also has the dubious distinction of being the first president to be replaced in office other than through succession due to a sitting president's death. His Vice President, Gerald Ford, who as ex-speaker of the House, filled the vice-president vacancy after Spiro Agnew, charged with income tax evasion, was forced to resign. Ford subsequently replaced Nixon as president.

The dark, violent aspect of our nation's presidency has reared its head on all too many occasions. In addition to our four martyred presidents, hopefuls Huey Long and Robert Kennedy were assassinated and attempts were made on the lives of Theodore Roosevelt, Franklin Roosevelt, Harry Truman, Ronald Reagan, Gerald Ford and George Wallace.

Primaries and Caucuses

Primaries mark a fast forward of a long and tedious candidate-selection process, which now can begin shortly after Inauguration Day. In choosing a national slate, the state primaries and caucuses, with all their shortcomings, offer a vast improvement over turbulent bygone days of big party bosses, smoke-filled rooms and national conventions' late hour wheeler-dealings.

Intrepid high office seekers often campaign a year or two early and then, beginning in January of the election year, after countless debates and campaign swings, learn their destiny at state caucuses and primaries after plunging millions of dollars—Governor Howard Dean spent $41 million in New Hampshire and Iowa alone—into TV commercials in hopes of winning the hearts and minds of voters.

Since 1952, New Hampshire has held the first-in-the-nation quadrennial primary as world attention focuses on a state with fewer than 500,000 registered voters. It is unquestionably the world's most thoroughly-covered election in proportion to the number of votes cast (averaging only 158,597 since 1952.)

Primary election and caucus pinback collections are especially enamored of the following campaigns: On two occasions, New Hampshire has proven forbidding territory by handing votes of no confidence to incumbent presidents: Harry Truman in 1952 and Lyndon Johnson in 1968. Both were plagued by unpopular wars in Asia and low standings in the polls prompted their announcement they would not seek re-election.

In contrast, the New Hampshire Primary propelled the long-shot candidacies of Senators Estes Kefauver, Eugene McCarthy and George McGovern into presidential runs that had to be taken seriously. The 2000 New Hampshire Primary saw Arizona Senator John McCain pull an upset over George W. Bush, the first time in 20 years that the state had not picked the ultimate winner in November.

A $2^1/_2$-inch multicolor "Veterans For Clark," showing the General in camouflaged mufti, and a "Lakes Region Supports Dean for America" 2¹/₂-inch pin picturing a sail-boat, offer refreshing departures from the predictable stars and stripes designs. Both figure to be keepers from the 2004 New Hampshire primary.

Third Parties

Third parties, over seventy in number, have been legally in existence since the early 1900s. Collecting third party memorabilia is a highly satisfying venture for the free-spirited. Regardless of their ideologies, third parties in-variably lack the inhibitions of the major parties when it comes to laying it on the line with unconventional and even outrageous positions. In most instances, third par-ties operate on a shoestring budget and are confronted with red tape, biased election laws and other roadblocks in many states in terms of getting on the ballot.

No third-party nominee has ever won the White House, or come close. A splinter candidate, however, *has* suc-ceeded in denying the presidency to a major party on a number of occasions, notably the 1912 Taft-Theodore Roosevelt-Wilson three-way race; George Wallace's Amer-ican Party in 1968 and more recently, Ralph Nader's Green Party in 2000. Buttons from these three cam-paigns are in great demand and well worth pursuing.

Specialists who collect by a specific campaign are known to seek out one jugate or example from each splinter party. Some of the more intriguing third-party candidates from the late nineteenth century are as follows:

The 1864 and 1872 campaigns were contested by one of political history's true eccentrics, George Francis Train, the People's Candidate. Train, or "The Citizen" as he pre-ferred to be called, was a millionaire founder of a steam packet service that brought Irish immigrants to America; part owner of the clipper ship *Flying Cloud,* and the inspi-ration for Phinneas Fogg in *Around the World in Eighty Days.* His platform endorsed woman's suffrage, hy-drotherapy and Turkish baths for public workers, plus im-peachment of Grant. Political artifacts relating to Train are scarce, a few lapel pins plus campaign flyers and calling cards, appropriately enough, dated from Blarney, Ireland.

Perennial lost-cause gadfly General Benjamin Franklin Butler accepted nominations for two parties at once in

1884—the Anti-Monopolists and the National Greenback party—after stalking out of the Democratic Convention when he was denied the presidential nomination.

Butler's drooping eyelid, generous paunch and look of an aging cherub were ripe for caricature and inspired a number of satiric trinkets portraying him in drag and various absurd costumes. Several lapel items reflect to Civil War days when as "Beast Butler," scourge of occupied New Orleans, he is said to have looted Southern mansions, absconding with a coffin filled with pilfered silverware. The incident earned the Union General another moniker, "Silver Spoons Butler" and several pins inscribed "Workingmen's Friends" feature the spoon device suspended from his medalet bust portrait. An even scarcer pinback shows Butler's bust sepiatone profile inside the bowl of a spoon.

The elite among Butler artifacts, an anti-Greenback figural cast-iron still bank, features a frog's body and Butler's face. He clutches a fistful of worthless paper currency with "For the Masses" embossed on one arm and "Bonds and Yachts for Me," referring to Butler's ownership of the famous yacht *America*.

The advent of the first women to run for president on the national ticket—Victoria C. Woodhull and Belva Ann Lockwood of the National Equal Rights Party—is discussed in the section, *Women Candidates*.

There's some credence to the theory that William Howard Taft's widely-publicized falling out with mentor Theodore Roosevelt precipitated the influx of third parties beginning in 1912. Roosevelt's celebrated exodus from the GOP convention that year led to the founding of a splinter party, the Bull Moose Progressives, that ultimately ripped asunder both parties and handed Woodrow Wilson the election. Taft's conservative stand in the White House, completely ignoring the will of the party and the people at large, succeeded in making third parties more enticing to working men, farmers, and other groups who felt slighted or completely ignored by the two major parties.

The Roosevelt-Johnson Bull Moosers rate antlers high with collectors, with 27 jugate varieties extant, up from only a dozen versions known at the time of the Don Warner sale in 1981. The 1912 campaign was abbreviated by a gentleman's agreement, following Roosevelt being wounded by a would-be assassin and the untimely passing of incumbent vice president James Sherman. Hailing from that woefully under-funded 1912 race, the jugates are highly uncommon and pricey. Fortunately a goodly number of other colorful Bull Moose buttons can still be obtained without hocking the family jewelry. These jugates, a carry-over from the Golden Age, come on as strong as the over-engined Roosevelt, and weigh heavily in our collective dreamscapes.

The Socialists had their own charismatic standard bearer in Eugene Victor Debs of Indiana, who headed the 1900, 1904, 1908, 1912, and 1920 slates. His best showing was in 1912 with 900,672 popular votes.

At the time of Debs' fifth presidential nomination by the Socialists in 1920, he was serving time for sedition in an Atlanta prison, a sentence imposed by Woodrow Wilson. In an article in the *APIC Keynoter*, Debs later stated: "an interesting question arose while we sat there in the warden's office (the night of the election) as to a pardon to myself in the event of winning the election." (Debs finished fourth.) Eugene Debs ranks on the A-list of presidential candidates in terms of collector popularity, as confirmed by APIC polls. His buttons, particularly those from the 1920 race, picturing him as a convict behind bars, command top dollar. So does a beautiful Debs-Hanford multicolor $1^{1}/4$-inch jugate with torch and clasped hands, one of the gems among a bumper crop of 1908 entries.

Next to the Socialists, 1908's biggest party, the Independence Party of New York, was founded by San Francisco newspaper magnate William Randolph Hearst. The party went national that year with Theodore Hisgen of Alabama and John Temple Graves of Georgia heading the slate. Though Hearst's own run for the presidency in 1920 was short-lived, his "The People's Candidate" portrait sepiatones are in great demand.

Collectors clamor for another dynamic third-party figure, "Fighting Bob" LaFollette of Wisconsin, who ran for president in 1924 under the newly-formed Republican

Progressive Party. LaFollette received almost a third as many votes as Calvin Coolidge and became the first third-party nominee of the century to win electoral votes, with 13. LaFollette appears on a $7/8$-inch multicolor jugate with Theodore Roosevelt, though the two were poles apart in ideology. A 1924 prized piece, a small brass teapot pin read, "LaFollette Did It," referring to his role in the Senate probe of the Harding scandals. A "C'mon Bob Let's Go" rebus button offered the option of LaFollette or a teapot.

Silas Swallow–George Carroll Prohibition Party pinbacks from the 1904 race rate high marks for their multicolor designs. A favorite $1^1/2$-inch classic play-on-words shows a pair of birds (as in swallows) with an American flag and a banner in beaks bears the homily "When The Swallows Homeward Fly/They Will Carroll Through the Sky/Down with the Bar Saloon and Still, Peace on Earth to Men Good Will/1904."

In 1948, Henry Wallace of the Progressive/American Labor party yielded a number of gems including "Wallace For President" in which the former vice president is shown in the shadow of FDR. Also in 1948 the States Rights Strom Thurmond–Fielding J. Wright buttons faithfully echo the reactionary stance of the Dixiecrats.

The candidacy of independent John Anderson on the National Unity ticket in 1980 includes a "America Needs Leadership," John Anderson–Patrick Lucey jugate; a Garry Trudeau "Doonesbury" cartoon pin worn by New Hampshire and Massachusetts primary volunteers pictures an Anderson aide and a voter who, glancing at an Anderson flyer says, "Never heard of him." The aide responds, "He's never heard of you either, just read it, okay?"

Also prized from the 1980 race are militant Angela Davis Communist Party "People Before Profits" and from 1984, "Rally With Davis–Gus Hall, Cobo Hall, Detroit, August 26" rectangular jugate.

Ross Perot, with his famous pie charts and homespun TV commercials, succeeded in building greater grass roots support for his Independent candidacy in 1992 than any challenger to the two-party system since Theodore Roosevelt. Among Perot's more evocative buttons are "A Choice Not a Change Perot-Stockdale/Vote Independent in 1992" jugate; a clever "Yeller Dawg" cartoon pin by Mike Peters, has Dawg muttering, "That Does It . . . I'm Voting For Perot." Another offbeat pin, a multicolor bust portrait of Van Gogh reads, "I'd give my other ear for Perot."

Vendor & Collector Buttons

One of the more explosive issues in the hobby is the validity of unofficial buttons produced by private vendors or collectors without the authorization of a campaign committee, political party or Political Action Committee (PAC).

Although in a sense, vendor-oriented political buttons have been around for a long time, and earlier versions were of superior quality and creativity, today's versions are generally humdrum and unimaginative. Hake's encyclopedias contain hundreds of vendor buttons without differentiating them as such.

The door really opened for vendor buttons in 1968 but the horse was already out of the barn as early as 1950 with the prime example: A ⁷/₈-inch Kennedy-Johnson jugate, regarded in most circles as being highly suspect. It still manages to bring top value, as does a known culprit, a 2¹/₂-inch "Prostitutes Vote for Nixon Or Kennedy/We Don't Care Who Gets In!" pin which usually goes for several hundred dollars. The 1968 race was infiltrated with hundreds of unofficial Nixon, Humphrey and George Wallace buttons, most of which merely tread water, remaining easily obtainable and available for pocket change.

The viability of the vendor button seriously came into question in 1972 when Thomas Eagleton, after a brief tenure as vice president on the Democratic slate, was asked by George McGovern to withdraw. Official jugates of the pair at that time were still very small in number, and suddenly were commanding $50 or more. Vendors stepped in and seized the opportunity for a quick turnover, flooding the market with new issues of the pair, thereby devaluing the originals to a piddling few dollars.

Vendor buttons have been known to stretch the limits as far as vulgarity and good taste are concerned, as witness the anti-Geraldine Ferraro items that proliferated in 1984 with reference to the female anatomy that no political party would dare to get away with.

We must confess that certain vendor issues can be both clever and amusing. For example, a Jim Bakker-Clinton jugate button, "Adulterous Blow-dried Televangelists For Clinton"; the anti-Nixon "I Have Nothing to Hide" cartoon of a nude Nixon flashing the V-sign, and the odds-on favorite from the 2000 campaign, G.W. Bush–Harry Potter jugate "Restore Wizardry to the White House."

The APIC regards vendor and collector issues as crass commercialism and has made strides to have them outlawed. The rules specify that no more than half of one percent of a collector's production may be used for selling or trading to other collectors. In certain other hobbies such as coins, stamps, videos, and CDs, private citizens who produce their own often land in prison.

On the other hand, many in the hobby feel that collectors have the right to collect anything they want and wonder what the fuss is all about. Lacking any kind of historical significance, these buttons offer no real incentive for the collector to invest in them.

Meanwhile, it is everyone's obligation to maintain a healthy skepticism about button origin.

THE ESSENTIALS

6

A PORTFOLIO OF BLUE RIBBON WINNERS

Bring on the drum roll ... strike up the band to "Hail To The Chief"—as a tribute to the most cherished stars in the political pinback diadem. This roll call of classics is based on a highly biased consensus among the movers and shakers in the political memorabilia field. We've included a value guide and Hake's coding system, the recognized reference for the hobby. These specimens are not necessarily easy to find—but hope springs eternal.

A. "Good Scales Teddy," 1904, Theodore Roosevelt–Alton Parker jugate; multicolor; 2 in. (Parker match) Hake 3138; $8,500.

B. "My Hobby A Winner" 1896 McKinley riding hobby-horse, multicolor, 2 in. Hake 290. (Bryan match); $5,000

C. Charles Evan Hughes–Charles Fairbanks no-name jugate; 1916, marked the last of bewhiskered candidates and passing of the Golden Era; multicolor; 1 1/4 in; Hake 59; $3,000.

D. "Four More years With Theodore"; 1904 classic Clifford Berryman cartoon pin of Roosevelt–Fairbanks with Teddy Bear; w, blk; 2 in.; Hake 3139; $3,000.

E. George McGovern sunset pop art design by Peter Max, 1972, br, blue, gr, blk, w.; 1 1/2 in.; Hake 2167; $400.

F. 1912 Roosevelt jugate; in splendid aqua, blk, r, w; 1 3/4 in.; Hake 33; and Taft–Wilson jugate match; $5,000.

G. H. Truman "8-Ball"; 1948 anti-Harry Truman pin inspired by gag gift symbol of tough luck presented HST at a Los Angeles Press Club roast; w, blk: 1 1/2 in. Hake 128; $10,000.

H. "I Wood-Row Wilson and Marshall to Victory/1912" arguably the top rebus pin of the 20th century; multicolor; 1 1/4 in. Hake 3081; $2,500.

I. "Give Me Hughes" 1916 Charles H. Hughes portrait with eagle, cannons, drum; flags: multicolor; r w, b, blk: Wilson match; $10,000.

J. Cox–Roosevelt "Sunburst Eagle" jugate; blk, w; 1 1/4 (also known in 7/8 in size); Hake 2009; $35,000.

K. 1908 William H. Taft–Sherman GOP a.k.a. Elephant Ears jugate, 1908; red, brown, yellow; 1 1/4 in. Hake 7; complements Bryan–Kern "Clean Sweep"; Hake 93; $2,500.

L. "Parker–Davis" 1904 "Shure Mike" jugate with Rooster in Uncle Sam costume; multicolored; 1 1/4 in; Hake 12; $750.

M. "Land on Washington" 1932 cartoon pun of Alf Landon circling Capital dome in airplane; red, white blueprint blue: 1 1/4; Hake 24; $2,500.

N. William J. Bryan 1896 "Our Standard Bearer/Two of America's Greatest Essentials To peace and prosperity";

Bryan portrait and ears of corn; brilliant tie-in to Bryan's native Nebraska; multicolor; 2 1/4 in. oval; Hake 124; $2,000.

O. Lyndon Johnson 1964 "Let Us Continue;" pairs LBJ and martyred John Kennedy one of the most poignant, effective modern pinbacks; b, blk; 1 3/4 in; $50.

Not pictured:
1896 "McKinley lunch box," "Do You Smoke/Yes, Since 1896/ That's What McKinley Promises;" key item extolling jobs and prosperity; multicolor; 2 in.; Hake 139; $3,500.

1912 Roosevelt–Johnson Progressive Bullmoose head with jugate portraits nesting in antlers: sepiatone; 1 1/4 in; Hake 3168; $6,000 plus. "Uncle Sam's 'White' Elephant/It's Game/It's Finish; 1904 Parker–Davis; uses sports and circus imagery and pun on GOP (Grand Old Pirate;) multicolor; 1 1/2 in.; Hake 112; $2,500. 1908 W. H. Taft portrait button with sentinel blowing trumpet; stunning classic by Maxfield Parish; multicolor; 1 1/2 in. Bryan match; Hake 119; $2,000 and up.

1920 "For President/Convict No. 9653" portrait of Socialist Eugene Debs behind bars; r, w, blk; Hake 15; $300, 1952 Dwight Eisenhower "Time For a Change/I Like Ike;" cartoon of baby with motto appearing on seat of diapers; w, b; 1 1/4 in.; Hake 108; $250.

1924 John Davis; "For President John Davis" sepiatone portrait with furled; r, w, b flags; 2 in. arguably the rarest of 20th Century candidates. Hake 200; $5,000.

Bryan Clock classic no-name button with dial set at sixteen minutes to one; 1900; an imaginative reference to free silver issue; pins; multicolor; 2 in. Hake 129; $750.

"The Spirit of the Republic/Success/1904 /President of All the People;" a. k. a. "Teddy at the Gate," one of the most expressive buttons to endorse equality; multicolor; 2 in. $5,500.

7
POLITICAL CAMPAIGNS 1789–2000

First Election—1789

President: George Washington   Uncontested
Vice President: John Adams
George Clinton (AF)
Thomas Jefferson (AF)
Aaron Burr (AF)

The term *election* here was a misnomer, as General George Washington was the unanimous choice of the first Electoral College convening in February 4, 1789, and the inaugural was more like a coronation. Washington received all 69 votes: there were no contesters, no campaigning, no oratory and no rush to the polls by the citizens of our fledgling nation.

Washington's absolute lock on the highest office was never to be duplicated again. Adams, however, as vice president, garnered only 34 votes as electors saw to it to cast one of their two votes for someone else as assurance the Father of Our County would not be upstaged. Congress agonized over a title for Washington (suggestions ranged from "His Excellency" to "His High Mightiest") and eventually settled for "Mr. President."

In the absence of campaign memorabilia to attract votes, Washington's first term produced some 50 varieties of inaugural items: brooches, cuff links and medalets and, most notably, metal clothing buttons or disks of brass, silvered, copper or pewter. Standout button designs are: "Long Live the President" encircling G.W. monogram in depressed center; G.W. with chains of 23 oval links encircling the initials of the states; and a bust of Washington and the Spread Eagle crested with sunburst.

Washington's ascension was further celebrated by a red and white cotton bandanna with cameo bust portraits of Washington, Adams, Jefferson, Franklin, Columbus and William Penn. Another textile treasure, possibly of Dutch origin, c. 1775–78, actually preceded Washington's presidency: A red linen kerchief of an equestrian General Washington with crossed flags and cannons, was reputedly printed at the request of his wife, Martha.

The British Battersea drapery tiebacks bearing bust images of Washington and at least two dye-transfer Liverpool tankards in his honor, may possibly be memorial or commemorative objects produced after his death.

Second Election—1792

President: George Washington (F)　　　　　Uncontested
Vice President: John Adams

Washington repeated as a unanimous choice, though he longed for retirement. But during his first term, a rift developed between cabinet members Alexander Hamilton and Thomas Jefferson. The "spirit of the party" as Washington called his fence-mending role, ultimately induced him to continue in office. He joined the Federalist party (as the Hamiltonians called themselves) but the Republicans, led by Jefferson, also gave Washington undivided support. Adams again ran a poor second, edging out devout Republican George Clinton 77–50.

The 1793 term apparently inspired only a pair of brass tokens featuring obverse military busts and rays beaming from a large eye past 15 stars to focus on the motto "Success to the United States." A medal struck for the second inaugural bearing a bust of Washington has rapidly escalated in value.

Washington, as an enduring national icon, continued to inspire memorial and commemorative events, including General Lafayette's 1824-25 return visit to the United States, the centennial of Washington's birth in 1832, the nation's centennial in 1876 and the 1932 bicentennial of his birth.

Third Election—1796

President: John Adams (F)
Vice President: Thomas Jefferson (DR)
Thomas Pinckney (F)
Aaron Burr (DR)

The first bona fide presidential campaign in our history evolved into a raucous shouting match. Paul F. Boller, Jr., in *Presidential Campaigns*, writes, "On both sides, bandbills, pamphlets and articles in party newspapers denounced, disparaged, damned, decried, denigrated and declaimed." Republicans carped over Adams's lack of confidence in the populace and preference for high-toned government. Federalists countered with accusations of Jefferson's sympathy with the French Revolution, calling him an "Atheist, coward, mountebank, trickster and toll of a foreign power."

Adams nosed out Jefferson by a narrow margin of three electoral votes. Up to this time, presidential electors were chosen by legislatures in some states before the practice of choosing electors by popular vote became nearly universal in 1828. This marks the first and only national election in which the president and vice president were of opposing parties, with Jefferson, the runner-up, occupying the second spot.

Adams's artifacts prove even more difficult to come by than those honoring Washington. The button made its first appearance: an engraved bust portrait of John Adams under glass in a looped pewter frame. A possibly unique leather bridle holder inscribed, "John Adams M.4, 1797" had been used on a horse that pulled

Adams's inaugural carriage. A pre-1880 ceramic rose jar, probably French, with black transfer busts of Adams and James Madison, is highly prized by collectors. An engraved portrait litho under glass in double frame is known as well as a pair of cuff links with Adams's bust incised and inscribed: *Jo Adams*. Both of these treasures may well be memorial items issued some time after his death in 1826. Of uncertain vintage, a coveted Liverpool creamware jug in blue with black-and-white checked borders shows a gilt bust portrait of Adams on the obverse and the warship *Orono* on the reverse.

Fourth Election—1800

President: Thomas Jefferson (DR)
Vice President: Aaron Burr (DR)
Defeated candidates:
John Adams (F)
John Jay (F)
Charles Pickney (F)

By a gnat's eyelash, Jefferson's Democratic Republicans insinuated themselves into office. The final tally was Jefferson 73, Burr 73 and Adams 65. The House of Representatives settled the deadlock with Jefferson squeaking by as victor amid a storm of controversy.

Disruption in Adams's own Federalist Party (the high Federalists or Hamiltonians had disowned him) clearly precipitated the second president's defeat at the hands of Jefferson.

Particularly controversial in Adams's unpopular term of office were his sponsorship of the Alien and Sedition Acts in 1878 and his appeasement tactics with France in negotiating the Treaty of Paris following the scandalous "XYZ" Affair. The first contest of highest office in the new century proved there could be a peaceful changing of the guard without shaking the foundations of the new republic.

Jefferson baubles and trinkets included an inaugural medalet profile bust image of the third president, which may be the first silver commemorative struck at the U.S. Mint. It was designed by John Reich as a model for a number of later Jefferson medals. Jefferson adorns a Liverpool pitcher; and creamware tankards are known with similar black transfer imagery. A key piece sums up the 1800 race: A hand-painted red, white and blue banner with oval portrait of Jefferson with eagle-scrolled motto, "T. Jefferson, President of the United States of American/John Adams No More." A Liverpoolware tankard depicting black transfer of Jefferson and a sailing vessel (perhaps the earliest use of the "ship of state" theme) commemorates his inaugural. Jefferson is pictured standing beside Washington's tomb in a stunning Staffordshire china piece following the General's passing in 1799.

Fifth Election—1804

President: Thomas Jefferson (DR)
Vice President: George Clinton (DR)
Defeated candidates:
Charles Pickney (F)
Rufus King (F)

Peace, prosperity, a reduction in the national debt, and the most momentous real estate buy of the century, the Louisiana Purchase of 1803, rendered our incumbent third president untouchable in the polls.

Attempts to sway voters during this period were limited largely to newspapers, pamphlets and oratory. A notable departure, a tankard image of Jefferson as a cow pulled in opposite directions by John Bull and Napoleon, satirized his difficulties with England and France during his second term.

Sixth Election—1808

President: James Madison (DR)
Vice President: George Clinton
Defeated candidates:
Charles Pickney (F)
Rufus King (F)

Following a Royal Navy attack of the American vessel Chesapeake in 1807, Jefferson's use of peaceful coercion, the Great Embargo (Federalists called it the "Dambargo") cut off trade with England and France. It became a major campaign issue by the Federalists; Pickney and King were overwhelmed 122 to 47 in electoral votes. Popular votes were not recorded until the 1824 race.

Again, as with any campaign items relating to the Founding Fathers, pickings are slim. A Liverpool creamer features a back transfer portrait of James Madison and a Scottish Chintz offers a medallion image of the fourth president. A true gem, a Liverpool pitcher, honors Madison's 1809 inauguration; "Hail Columbia, Happy Land," celebrates Jefferson's Victory in "Revolution of l800." Madison made a belated cameo appearance in a small embossed "Eight Presidents Medal" engraved in l840. A rather crudely rendered image of Madison appears on silk ribbon.

Seventh Election—1812

President: James Madison (DR)
Vice President: Eldridge Gerry
Defeated candidates:
DeWitt Clinton, Jared Ingersoll (Ran as Clintonians, a coalition of Republicans and Federalists.)

"Mr. Madison's War," the War of 1812, was the central issue in this race. No president has ever failed to be re-elected in wartime, and Madison, no exception, won handily, 128 to 89. Our fourth president is pictured on at least a half dozen bandannas commemorating the War of 1812.

Eighth Election—1816

President: James Monroe (DR)
Vice President: Daniel Tompkins (DR)

The 8th election was not a true presidential campaign, although Rufus King, backed by the Federalists, made a half-hearted challenge.

Victor in the War of 1812, Madison's sponsorship of a national bank and higher import duties to protect America's industries assured the incumbent a landslide 183–34 victory over King. The Republican win sounded the Federalist's death knell and set the stage for Madison's heir-apparent, James Monroe.

A cherished remembrance from 1816 is a set of English gaming tokens inscribed "Munro" (sic) with eagle and olive branches. A few tiny 3-inch-high ceramic mugs with floral decoration and "Monroe" inscribed are known as well as a ceramic bust portrait tankard in black or blue transfer, a mere 2$^{1}/_{2}$ inches high.

Ninth Election—1820

President: James Monroe (DR)   Uncontested
Vice President: Daniel Tompkins

Monroe and his running mate Tompkins returned to high office with the most lopsided victory in history, capturing 231 of 232 electoral votes. The lone holdout,

William Plumer, a former New Hampshire senator and governor, cast his vote for Secretary of State John Quincy Adams.

A Vieux Paris porcelain demitasse cup in Monroe's image is one of the few mementos from his second term.

Tenth Election—1824

President: John Quincy Adams (NR)
Vice President: John Calhoun
Defeated candidates:
Andrew Jackson (D)
Henry Clay (DR)
William H. Crawford (DR)

In a close, hotly-contested election, Jackson outpolled John Adams's son, John Quincy Adams, 99 to 84 and for the first time, popular votes were counted with Jackson again ahead 153,544 to 108,740. Calhoun was elected vice president by gaining more than two-thirds of the votes cast. By the terms of the 12th Amendment, Senate and House, in joint session, declared that no candidate had received a first-place majority and Adams was declared winner by one ballot. Jacksonians went ballistic as they felt that Adams and Henry Clay, who had tilted the House vote, had struck a "corrupt bargain." Suspicion was further roused when Adams appointed Clay as Secretary of State. Jackson resigned from the Senate; in 1825, vengeful Old Hickory headed home to the Hermitage to embark on an all-out campaign seeking vindication by winning the 1828 race.

The 1824 race produced the first widely-circulated items actually used prior to election day and did much to establish the cult of personality in national politics. It encompassed three different brass medalets of Jackson, with his portrait and inscription ballyhooing the Major General's victory in the Battle of New Orleans and the Congressional Medal of Honor awarded for his military prowess. The first silk bandannas featuring presidential candidates were probably used by Jackson in 1824, also recalling his heroics at New Orleans and successful Florida military campaigns in 1819. Inspiring lively controversy as to date of and attribution to his 1824 bid, a New Haven, Connecticut, earthenware crock features a large incised sailing sloop with the motto "15,000 Majority GNL Jackson." Both a rust-red pitcher and plate date bearing Jackson's bust image is dated as 1824, or possibly earlier.

John Quincy Adams's likeness appears on a papier-mache snuffbox, a litho paper under glass in pewter frame pendant and at least four versions of stencil-slo-gan thread boxes.

11th Election—1828

President: Andrew Jackson (D)
Vice President: John C. Calhoun
Defeated candidates:
John Quincy Adams (NR)
Benjamin Rush (NR)

Revenge was sweet as Jackson trounced John Quincy Adams 178 to 83 in the electoral vote and 647,286 to 508,064 in the popular vote.

Jackson supporters characterized this campaign as a struggle "between the democracy of the country on one hand, a lordly purse-proud aristocracy on the other." In a venomous, mud-slinging campaign, Jackson was ac-cused of multiple murders (alleging that during the Creek War, he approved the execution of six deserters); also that he lived in sin with his beloved Rachel. Jack-sonites countered by accusing "arch-Puritan Adams" of having procured young American virgins for the Russian tsar.

A prized French thread box inscribed "Jackson and no corruption" is the sole reminder of the rankling 1824 deadlock and run-off. Another thread box titled "Old Hickory Forever" and a "General Andrew Jackson" trin-ket box are known. A superb bronze statuette of a youthful, beardless Jackson is highly prized. A pendant with litho Jackson image with flowing mane and coat collar up and wide open in pewter frame, is a match to an early John Quincy Adams entry. Adams's relics in-cluded an unusual redware tile of the full-standing sixth president, in the form of a hand-carved wooden bread mold and an ornate French velvet thread box which opens to display his bust images. An anti-Jackson woodcut "Bloody Deeds of General Jackson" depicting coffin silhouettes, dredge up the infamous Creek War incident.

12th Election—1832

President: Andrew Jackson
Vice President: Martin Van Buren
Defeated candidates:
Henry Clay (DR) and John Sargeant
William Wirt (AM) and Amos Ellmaker
John Floyd (D) and Henry Lee

For the first time in the history of the young Republic, a president took a stand on a social issue by vetoing the re-chartering the Second Bank of the United States, and then looked to voters in 1832 to give their stamp of approval. Jackson believed that specie, gold or silver, not paper money, should serve as the standard medium of exchange. "No Bank! Down with the Rag Money" was a typical Jackson campaign slogan. Our seventh president received a rousing endorsement at the polls as he triumphed over Henry Clay 329 to 49 and won the popular vote 687,502 to 530,189.

A classic anti-Jackson broadside pictured the seventh president wearing a crown and royal robes: "King Andrew the First/Born to Command/Shall He Reign Over Us, Or Shall the People Rule?" Clay's strategy did not pay off in depicting Jackson as one who rules by whim rather than adhering to constitutional principles. A vibrant "National Currency Revenue and Protection" Clay-clad banner succinctly limns the National Republican platform.

13th Election—1836

President: Martin Van Buren (D)
Vice President: Richard Johnson
Defeated candidates:
William Henry Harrison (W) and Francis Granger
Hugh White (W)
Willie Mangum (I)

Jackson's firm stand on blocking South Carolina's bid to nullify the tariff laws, alienated Southern states' rights advocates. National Republicans were still chafing over his withdrawing government funds and packing them in state banks and voting for the 1832 bill that would have re-chartered the Bank of the United States also; as well as his stance against high tariffs. Southerners distrusted Van Buren as Jackson's choice as successor, dismissing him as a slick New Yorker. The Whigs, too disorganized to hold a national convention, settled for a ticket of three favorite sons from various sections of the country.

William Henry Harrison, an anti-Masonic Whig and the strongest of the three, pulled 73 of the 124 electoral votes to Van Buren's rousing 170 votes. The popular vote was 762,678 for Van Buren to 549,508 for Harrison. Martin Van Buren became the first president who had not been a British subject.

A deep blue and copper lusterware pitcher with transfer of Martin Van Buren tops collectors' lists and the successful nominee's impeccable visage adorns a papier-mache snuffbox. He is shown in bust profile on a handsome "Van Buren Democrat" sulphide cameo brooch. A satirical cartoon, "Political Race Course" depicts Harrison as a racehorse with human face pacing the 1836 contenders.

14th Election—1840

President: William Henry Harrison (W)
Vice President: John Tyler
Defeated candidates:
Martin Van Buren (D)
Richard Johnson
James G. Birney (L)*

Harrison's "Tippecanoe and Tyler Too" campaign set a new standard of image-building that remains a practical model even today. For the first time, the populace was treated to barbecues, parades and rallies. A deluge of walking sticks, broadsides, kerchiefs and lapel devices helped reshape the aging war hero Harrison's persona. Whig constituents transformed an off-hand slur by Henry Clay (who'd been passed by in Harrison's favor) giving Harrison a new moniker "the log cabin hard cider candidate."

15th Election—1844

President: James Knox Polk
Vice President: George M. Dallas
Defeated Candidates:
Henry Clay (W) and Theodore Frelinghuysen
James G. Birney (L)*

The pivotal campaign issue in 1844 was territorial expansion. Re-annexation of Texas, originally part of the Louisiana Territory, threatened to trigger war with Mexico. Many in the North opposed annexation as it meant adding a sizable slave territory.

*The Liberty Party antislavery spin-off—forerunner of the Free Soil Party of the 1840s and the Republican Party of the 1850s.

The Democrats shrewdly linked Texas with Oregon as a national vs. sectional expansionist target, thereby dodging the slavery issue. Under the stirring slogan "Fifty-Four Forty Or Fight," all of Oregon was claimed, extending to Alaska's southern boundary (54 degrees 40'). John Tyler, who filled out William Henry Harrison's term of office, did not run. James Polk, chosen by the Democrats, was a former House speaker (1835-39) and governor of Tennessee from 1839–41. Pennsylvanian George Dallas formerly served as ambassador to Russia. Derisively called "Polk the Plodder" by the Whigs, he still forged ahead to become eleventh U.S. president. Polk edged rival Henry Clay by a narrow margin, winning the popular vote 1,275,016 to 1,129,102; electoral count: 170 to Clay's 105.

The Whigs blamed their defeat on James Birney who siphoned off votes that might have gone to Clay. Polk proved to be an imaginative and decisive leader.

Collector's Choice

Polk memorabilia is sparse. A Polk–Dallas jugate ribbon shows the Lone Star of Texas and the slogan "Alone But Not Deserted" and "Clear the Way for Old Kentucky, I'm That Same Old Coon" a cartoon ribbon of a sly raccoon on a fence rail, which proved prophetic as again Clay straddled the slavery issue.

Introduced in 1844, looped "shell" lapel ornaments were stamped from thin brass sheets; also pewter rimmed lapel devices with paper images of Polk and Clay.

Also a first were multicolored (in many cases hand-tinted) lithographed prints of the candidates and running mates by Nathanial Currier of NYC and E.B. Kellog and E.C. Hanmer of Hartford which were peddled to the masses for about fifteen cents apiece. The Currier lithos, known as Grand National Banners, were popular up through the Lincoln years.

16th Election—1848

President: Zachary Taylor (W)
Vice President: Millard Fillmore
Defeated candidates:
Lewis Cass (D) and William Butler
Martin Van Buren and Charles Francis Adams (Free Soil Party)

"Old Zack" Taylor's military credentials were far more impressive than Old Tippecanoe's. However, only a gifted orator such as Abraham Lincoln, then in the House of Representatives, could make a virtue out of General Taylor's vagueness on issues. By 1848, the slavery issue was clearly a "ticking time bomb." The Democrats' Lewis Cass advocated "squatter sovereignty," the right of federal territory settlers to decide the slavery questions on their own.

Taylor opposed slavery expansion in the West. In the battle between two generals, the Whigs were victorious, 163 to 127, with a slim popular vote edge of 1,360,099 to 1,220,544. Martin Van Buren's Free Soilers garnered 291,263 votes or 10% of the total and probably cost Cass the election by taking away anti-slavery votes, especially outside of New York State.

Taylor served only one year in office before being fatally stricken with gastroenteritis and his vice president, Millard Fillmore, succeeded him.

Collector's Choice

The Whig party's last successful presidential campaign was memorialized by a vibrant N. Currier Grand National Banner with jugate portraits of Taylor and Fillmore. General Taylor was immortalized in a bas-relief cast-iron parlor stove and his prowess in the Mexican War was played up heavily in ribbons and bandannas. Collectors cherish at least five Taylor lithographed hanging buttons in pewter frames with images of vice president Millard Fillmore on the reverse. A favorite reads, "General Taylor Never Surrenders." A match for Lewis Cass with William Butler on reverse is known, as is a small brass shellback bearing his bust profile.

17th Election—1852

President: Franklin Pierce (D)
Vice President: William King
Defeated candidates:
Winfield Scott (W) and John Graham
John Parker Hale (FS)

The fourteenth president, another ex-Mexican War general, Democratic Dark Horse Franklin Pierce of New Hampshire, and his running mate William Rufus DeVane King, pinned a stunning defeat on General "Old Fuss 'n' Feathers" Winfield Scott and his vice-president nominee William Graham, a North Carolinian who at the time served as secretary of the Navy under Fillmore.

Pierce supported the Compromise of 1850, with its notorious Fugitive Slave Act, more vigorously than did Taylor. The stirring Democrat slogan, "We Polked 'em in '44/We'll Pierce 'em in '52" rang true. The result was humiliating to the Whigs: Pierce polled 1,601,474 to Taylor's 1,386,580; the electoral margin was 254 to 42 as the Whigs carried only four states. The Whigs slipped into further decline and were soon to disappear as an independent force in American politics.

As for King, the Alabaman is best remembered as the vice president who never served. Seriously ill with tuberculosis when nominated, he died before assuming office, leaving a vacancy that was unfilled until the '56 election. The rather effete King, who effected a wig long after they were out of fashion, was frequently referred to by Andrew Jackson as "Miss Nancy."

Collector's Choice

Pierce's campaign may be remembered by several superb ribbons: A $6^1/_2$-in. jugate of Pierce and King with facsimile signatures; a "We Honor the Citizen and Soldier, General Franklin Pierce" portrait ribbon; and also a number of medalets. A pennant medallion with embossed full-torso image shows the nominee brandishing a rolled-up document. A prized match safe portrays General Scott in profile wearing a cockade hat. Scott, ever enamored of fancy uniforms, strikes a classic pose holding the reins of a prancing steed in a r, w, br, bandanna. The grizzled war hero appears out of place on a 5-inch diameter ABC plate.

18th Election—1856

President: James Buchanan (D)
Vice President: John C. Breckinridge
Defeated candidates:
John C. Fremont (R) and William Dayton
Millard Filmore (A) and Andrew Donelson

The enactment of the Kansas-Nebraska Act of 1854 and a bloody civil war in Kansas between free-soilers and pro-slavery settlers, precipitated the schism between the two major parties in this pivotal campaign.

On February 28, 1854, the Republican Party as we know it today was born in a little schoolhouse in Ripon, Wisconsin. At first a sectional party, noticeably lacking in Southern support, the Republicans pledged to oppose further extension of slavery and protested the Kansas–Nebraska

Act. The Democrats took the opposite position, vowing to resist all attempts toward reviving, in or out of Congress, the agitation of the slavery issue.

A third party, the "No-Nothings," an offshoot of a secret society organized in New York in 1849, directed its prejudices against aliens, particularly Irish immigrants, and was anti-Catholic as well. The "No Nothings," weakened by defections to the new Republican ranks in 1855, nominated ex-president Millard Fillmore and Andrew J. Donelson to run under a new American Party banner.

The Republicans chose the "Pathfinder" General John Fremont of California, renowned for his explorations in the Far West; his running mate was William L. Dayton, a former Whig senator from New Jersey, who opposed the Compromise of 1850.

The Democrats selected James "Old Buck" Buchanan of Pennsylvania, a Secretary of State under Polk and a former minister to England, and John C. Breckinridge of Kentucky who had served in both the House and Senate.

Buchanan pulled 174 electoral votes vs. 114 for Fremont, the ominous aspect being that all but a handful of Republican votes came from non-slaveholding states. Fillmore won 25 percent of the popular vote at 874,534, but carried only one state, Maryland, with eight electoral votes. Buchanan, the first and only bachelor president, kept a low profile throughout the 1856 campaign and stayed at his country estate in Lancaster, Pennsylvania and occasionally received visitors.

Collector's Choice

Fremont campaign items might well have led to their political doom in 1856—as with one exception, they stridently implied "a damn the south and damn the consequences" theme. The lone departure was a ribbon pledging "According To The True Spirit Of The Constitution . . . To Preserve Both Liberty and Union."

A classic banner for the 1856 race is an anti-Buchanan "Buck & Breck/Border Ruffian/Democracy & Slavery" showing a chained black slave astride a lamb. A huge broadside with oval portraits of Buchanan and Breckinridge flanking George Washington, topped by large eagle and Miss Liberty, lists the full Democratic slate. An unusual tiny pillbox has an embossed Buchanan portrait. A clever uniface brass shellback showing a deer, as in "Buck" and a cannon barrel as in "Cannon," to complete the name rebus, rates as one of the key mid-nineteenth century campaign items.

A trio of ribbons personify the Fremont candidacy: A black on pale mint-green portrait ribbon, with name misspelled "Jonn" and the "Free Spoil, Free Speech, Fremont" entry. "Fremont-Dayton Black Republican" anti-Republican piece illustrates a runaway slave above a black skull and crossbones, a coveted 3-D entry, a tin parade lantern, shows Fillmore-Donelson in pierced letters on the door.

A choice pun-filled ribbon reads: "We Po'ked 'em in '44,We Pierced 'em in 52, And We'll Buck 'em' in '56."

19th Election—1860

President: Abraham Lincoln (R)
Vice President: Hannibal Hamlin
Defeated Candidates:
Stephen A. Douglas (DN) and Herschell Johnson
John C. Breckinridge (DS) and Joseph Lane
John Bell (CU) and Edward Everett
Confederate States of America: 1861

Jefferson Davis and Alexander Stevens were elected by the C.S.A.

The Dred Scott decision by the U.S. Supreme Court in 1857 that slavery was legal in all territories angered Republicans and split the Democrats, further fueling the heat of sectional tensions. Stephen A. Douglas, who refused to endorse a pro-slavery program, headed the Democrats. The southern Democrat wing walked out of the convention and later nominated John C. Breckinridge, vice president under Buchanan. Breckinridge was endorsed by former presidents, Buchanan, Tyler and Pierce. Republicans chose Abraham Lincoln of Illinois, the Rail-Splitter candidate, who'd gained a groundswell of support from the plains people of the West. The Constitution Party, whose one fervent concern was the preservation of the Union, nominated House Speaker John Bell.

Lincoln won decisively, outpolling his three opponents combined, with 180 to 72 edge over second-place Breckinridge; Bell posted 39 votes and Stephen Douglas 12.

The popular count read Lincoln 1.8 million, Stephen Douglas 1.4, Breckinridge 847,953 and John Bell 590,631.

Collectors Choice

Matching ferrotypes and striking jugate ribbons feature all four candidates. Inspired by 1860 torchlight parades, a "Old Abe/Ich Mein Prince of Rails" triangular transparency appealed to German-American voters and a handmade wood "Fear Not/Old Abe Is Our Leader," Rail-Splitter's ax parade standard. A gilded brass-framed oval $2^1/_2$ x $2^1/_8$ in. ambrotype of a beardless Lincoln, ranks as the king among lapel pins. More medals and medalets were struck in Lincoln's honor than for any other commander-in-chief. His two campaigns and untimely passing precipitated a rash of examples when political medalets were at their zenith.

A number of Lincoln-Hamlin flag banners and ribbons give collectors an adrenaline high. Renderings of the frontier's zig-zagging split-rail fences (a brainchild of Lincoln's longtime friend Richard Oglesby) remind voters of "Honest Abe's" humble beginning as a splitter of rails and implied sympathy with ordinary folk. Closely akin to the Rail-Splitter theme was the selling of Lincoln as a westerner. Numerous tokens hailed him as "Honest Abe of the West/The Hannibal of America."

Parade banners, noisemakers, and torches from "The Wide Awakes," a pro-Lincoln paramilitary volunteer corps, also have special appeal.

While Lincoln campaign objects often focused on Republican aversion to the volatile issue of slavery, the general tenor remained multi-faceted and non-confrontational. These items reflected regional priorities and were rather subdued in style except in safe, staunchly anti-slavery constituencies.

John Bell's run is known for a number of rebus ribbons picturing a bell; N. Currier Grand National Banner pictures standing figures Bell and Edward Everett holding up a copy of the Constitution.

Stephen Douglas items, tokens in particular, made the case for popular sovereignty (i.e.) "Nonintervention/Popular Soverty (sic)"; and the wordy "Vox Populi, Vox Dei/The Voice of the people is the Voice of God/let it Be

Heard Let All Obey/with these Political maxims For Our Guide/The Union of the States Will Be Perpetual." Another Douglas token made the plea, "Support 'The Little Giant' Who has Proved Himself the Greatest Statesman of the Age."

An unabashed Breckenridge appeal for Southern votes read, "No Submission to the North" with "The Wealth of the South/Rice, Tobacco, Sugar, Cotton," on the medal's reverse.

Often hailed as hobby's supreme lapel item—an 1864 Abraham Lincoln-Andrew Johnson brass shell shield ferrotype.

20th Election—1864

President: Abraham Lincoln (R)
Vice President: Andrew Johnson
Defeated candidates:
George McClellan and George Pendleton (D)

Ironically, as the 1864 race was winding down, Lincoln appeared at the brink of defeat. His opponent, ex-Commander-in-Chief of the Union Forces, Pennsylvanian General George McClellan, was deeply hurt when Lincoln replaced him in 1862 citing indecisiveness and failure to follow through after a bloody victory at Antietam. McClellan's running mate was Ohio congressman George Pendleton.

Hannibal Hamlin served as a private in the Maine Coast Guard for sixty days. Lincoln considered Hamlin's views of reconstruction of the postwar South as too severe, turning instead in 1864 to Andrew Johnson, a war Democrat from Tennessee.

From the war front, however, resounding victories by Generals Ulysses S. Grant and William T. Sherman and the Admiral David Farragut's capture of Mobile Bay and defeat of the CSA's flotilla at New Orleans dramatically transformed the political picture.

Lincoln's margin of victory was even more convincing as he ran up 212 electoral votes to McClellan's 21, although the popular count was closer, 2.2 million to 1.8. Lincoln accepted the landslide win as a mandate for restoration of the Union and the abolition of slavery. A *Harper's*

Weekly cartoon proclaimed "Long Live Abraham Lincoln a Little Longer."

Lincoln's second term was all too brief; he was assassinated by John Wilkes Booth in 1865 just five days after CSA's General Robert E. Lee surrendered to Grant at Appomattox.

Johnson's embarrassing inaugural tirade while reportedly inebriated, admonished fellow senators to remember their debt to the common men who had put them in office. It was not a glorious start for the second Lincoln administration.

Collector's Choice

Few 1864 campaign items bothered to exploit the politics of personality as instead, both parties focused primarily on the Union and victory. Most of the forty-five known McClellan tokens portrayed him in military bust design; two others were in equestrian poses. Human rights were a major Lincoln theme in 1864. A token pledged, "If I Am Reelected president Slavery Must be Abolished with the Reunion of States"; Others read "Proclaim Liberty Throughout the Land," "Liberty ForAll/1864." The Democrats castigated Lincoln for fomenting the war and his failure to win it. An inflammatory McClellan broadside warned that a "Black Republican" victory would result in "negro Equality" and other grim results.

The 1864 Lincoln-Johnson ferrotype jugate shield ranks as the most elusive of all pre-1896 jugate pins. As dealer Dave Frent pointed out in 1998 in selling the shield, "When compared to a Cox/Roosevelt jugate celluloid button, this item is twenty to thirty times rarer." It scaled to new heights at $38,500.

21st Election—1868

President: Ulysses S. Grant (R)
Vice President: Schuyler Colfax
Defeated candidates:
Horatio Seymour (D)
Gen. Francis P. Blair

Andrew Johnson, who had completed Lincoln's second term of office to become the 17th president, was in trouble from the beginning; he openly clashed with the Radical Republicans who wished to punish the Confederate states more severely than Johnson and Lincoln deemed necessary. When Johnson dismissed Secretary of War Edwin Stanton, who refused to resign, the Senate felt certain it had solid ground for impeachment—better grounds than suggested by his enemies, of insanity or whiskey. Johnson was charged with "high crimes and misdemeanors" and is our only president to be impeached. Actually, the two-thirds vote needed to convict failed by one vote as seven Republican senators sacrificed their careers to vote in Johnson's favor.

Ironically, six years after leaving office, Johnson was re-elected to the Senate and was warmly received with applause in the Senate Chamber and flowers at his desk.

The 1868 campaign focusing on the ending of the Civil War and its impact on reconstruction was one of the most lackluster in history. War hero Ulysses Grant of Illinois and Schuyler Colfax of Indiana, a member of the House of Representatives, led the Republican slate; for the Dems, they tapped Horatio Seymour, a former Governor of New York, who was so reluctant to accept the nomination, he was called "The Great Decliner"; Gen. Francis P. Blair, of Missouri, one of the founders of the Free Soil Party in 1848, and later served on Gen. Sherman's staff, eagerly accepted the second-place slot.

Grant declined to actively campaign, making only one brief Western tour with fellow generals Sherman and Sheridan. The black vote proved to be critical as Grant, who was accused of trying to Africanize the South, faced formidable sectional opposition. Final tally in the electoral college was Grant 214, Seymour 80. The Democrat's popular vote margin was 3 million to 2.7. Listed as not voting were the unreconstructed states: Mississippi, Texas and Virginia.

Collector's Choice

Round gutta percha embossed-jugate snuffboxes representing both Republican and Democrat slates, other tobacco-related accessories and whimsical toys and novelties enrich a wide variety of some 200, 1868 campaign artifacts, less than half the quantity of the losing Democrats. Grant, usually in military regalia, appears on elaborate shell badges and nearly every known variety of medalet and lapel pins. A collector favorite is a figural hinged-brass pin of an army knapsack that opens to reveal a bust portrait of the general. Countless ribbons and banners bear Grant's conciliatory "Let us have peace." A medalet depicts stacked muskets and a vignette of a former Confederate plowing a field, which reads, "The Men Will Need Their Horses to Plow With/Appomattox."

Few 1868 Democrat objects exploit issues or symbolism of any sort, although a prized Horatio Seymour parade flag espouses "paper currency . . . equal taxation and government of the people." A stunning Currier & Ives National Banner with jugate portraits of Seymour-Blair champions "Peace, Union and Constitutional Government" and a pair of vignettes show hands pushing a plow and a flexed arm wielding a hammer. A favorite figural brass shell pin portrays an eagle in flight with a Seymour portrait shield pendant in its beak.

22nd Election—1872

President: Ulysses Grant
Vice President: Henry Wilson
Defeated candidates:
Horace Greeley (D)
George Pendleton (D)
Thomas Hendricks (ID)

The 1872 race is considered by historians as one of the most embarrassing elections in history. "Deciding between Grant and Greeley," lamented statesman Alexander Stephens, was a choice between "hemlock and strychnine." Grant's first term introduced the derogatory epithet "Grantism" to the lexicon. It entailed nepotism, the spoils system and shocking corruption in high office. Vice president Schuyler Colfax retired in disgrace after the Credit Mobilier scandal (this spin-off of the Union Pacific bribed Colfax with large blocks of stock). Grant's private secretary General Orville Babcock was part of a "Whiskey Ring" that defrauded the government of millions of taxes. While Grant himself was never implicated, his choice of appointees was suspect.

The Republican standard bearer, Horace Greeley, an editor of the *New York Tribune,* was influential in nominating Lincoln in 1860 and credited with hastening the Emancipation Proclamation with publication of his "Prayer of Twenty Millions." Greeley's running mate,

George Pendleton of Ohio had earlier tasted defeat as McClellan's vice-presidential candidate in 1864.

Greeley mounted a strong speaking campaign but was considered by many as a lifelong gadfly of radical Republican causes. The Republicans were also woefully short of funds. Grant carried all but six states with a popular vote of 3.6 million vs. 2.8 for his opponent. Electorally, the gap was wider, 286 to 66. Greeley, exhausted and devastated by the defeat and the death of his wife shortly before the election, was relieved of his editorial post by *Tribune* owner, Whitelaw Reid. Greeley's mind snapped; he was institutionalized and died before the end of November.

Collector's Choice

Unaccountably, outrage over the shabby scandals of Grant's first term—the single, unifying link between Democrats and idealistic Republican defectors, was never exploited in campaign items (the lone exception being a "Reform 1872" brass badge). A number of tokens and shell badges deify Greeley as "The Honest Farmer of Chappaqua," and the "Sage of Chappaqua." A favorite button, a gilded figural quill pen attests, "The Pen Is Mightier Than The Sword," obliquely touting his editorial prowess over Grant's militarism.

A slyly satirical cardboard fan caricature of Greeley with wisps of cotton to simulate his side-whiskers, features scathing cartoons on the fan's reverse; captioned in one panel "What I Know About Farming," a pair of mules are shown kicking Greeley over the plowshare.

The trademark Greeley parsons hat is embodied in a cast-iron match safe, an ivory Stanhope telescope, and a number of badges and chintzes. A Greeley hat suspended from a figural clasped hands badge, symbolizes sectional reconciliation and an end to Radical Reconstruction.

Author and historian Roger Fisher writes that the Greeley artifacts spelled "the last of a generation of campaign items reflecting our preoccupation with the politics of sectional conflict."

For the Republicans, as an appeal to the blue collar vote, a Currier & Ives litho "Workingman's Banner," identifies

Grant plying his trade as "The Galena Tanner" and Wilson as "The Natick Shoemaker." Grant and Wilson are pictured on at least a half-dozen uniface ferrotype jugates.

23rd Election—1876

President: Rutherford B. Hayes (R)
Vice President: William A. Wheeler
Defeated candidates:
Samuel Tilden (D) and Thomas Hendricks

The U.S. centennial campaign produced more than its share of fireworks. Samuel Tilden, a New York district attorney who had sent Tammany's Boss Tweed and his hoodlums to prison, led the reform-minded Democrats with Thomas Hendricks, a former senator and governor of Indiana, as running mate.

Republicans countered the "Tilden and Reform!" rallying cry with "Hurrah! For Hayes and Honest Ways." Civil War General Rutherford B. Hayes, a three-time Ohio governor, was paired with William Wheeler, a New York member of the House of Representatives

The bitterest, longest and most controversial presidential race in history ensued, rivaled only by the G.W. Bush-Al Gore fracas in the year 2000.

Every plank of the Democrat's platform began "Reform is necessary . . . " and indeed with the dirt exposed from Grant's eight years in office, the odds of a Republican win were slim. The Hayes forces effectively "waved the bloody shirt," by charging that every man that shot Union soldiers was a Democrat and "the man who assassinated Lincoln was also a Democrat."

Tilden, who did not really want the presidency and was in poor health, refused to wage a vigorous campaign. It still appeared that Tilden had won, as the first returns rolled in. The votes of three Southern states and Oregon were doubtful. In South Carolina, Florida and Louisana, still under carpetbag rule, the election board had thrown out thousands of Democratic votes on the grounds of fraud and intimidation. Tilden received a quarter of a million more popular votes, 4.3 to 4 million and topped Hayes electorally 184 to 165, only one vote shy of victory. It finally came down to 20 disputed votes in the South. Congess set up a 13-member electoral commission and dispatched to the disputed states.

Samuel Elliot Morrison in the *Oxford History of the American People*, writes, "There seems no doubt that a deal was made by the GOP and Southern Democrat leaders, by virtue of which, in return for their acquiescence in Hayes's election, they promised on his behalf to withdraw the garrison and wink at non-reinforcement of Amendment XV, guaranteeing civil rights to the freedman. The bargain was kept by both sides."

The recount read Hayes 185, Tilden 184. No attempt was made to enforce Amendment XV until the Franklin D. Roosevelt administration.

Collector's Choice

Hayes's candidacy inspired the last of the presidential papier-mache snuffboxes to appear in the post Civil War era. Only $2^1/2$ in. in diameter, it features jugate busts of Hayes-Wheeler. An anti-Tilden token portrays a coffin atop a bier, with the epitaph "Here Lies Our Little Tilden Dear/He Died of Reform 'Loquendi-Rhoea' " (verbal diarrhea). Brass shellback Hayes favorites included a jugate shield entry inscribed "Centennial Candidates for 1876."

One-design-fits-all for both parties again prevailed. Except for the changing of the jugate guard, a gilded winged eagle button with ribbon and suspended Hayes-Wheeler imagery looks predictably similar to a 20-year span of Gilded Age issues expressing fealty for Republican nominees James Blaine, James Garfield, and Benjamin Harrison.

Solid celluloid buttons were introduced in '76 and enjoyed a brief vogue until they give way to the celluloid-layered tin versions a decade later. Highly prized and colorful for a change, matching red, white and blue jugate campaign banners for both parties are topped with a "Centennial" portrait of George Washington.

24th Election—1880

President: James Abram Garfield (R)
Vice President: Chester Allan Arthur
Defeated candidates:
Winfield Scott (D) and William H. English
James Weaver (GL) and James Field

A liberal "dark horse," 48-year-old Ohio congressman and military hero, James Garfield, was picked on the thirty-sixth ballot as the Republican headliner in '80; his running mate, Chester A. Arthur, a New York gentleman boss, had been fired by Hayes from his lucrative post as collector of the New York Port Authority several years earlier, as a start toward cleaning up graft in the civil service.

The Democrats chose another Civil War general, a fair-minded military governor of Texas and Louisiana in 1868, Winfield Scott Hancock. Wealthy Indiana banker William H. English ran in the second slot.

It was a relatively humdrum contest compared with the frenetic '76 affair. Both parties endorsed civil-service reform, opposed government aid to parochial schools and limiting Chinese immigration. Republicans touted Garfield's rags-to-riches rise from a log cabin and nicknamed him "Boatman Jim" for his stint on the Ohio canal as a boy. His campaign was largely limited to receiving visitors at his Mentor, Ohio home to listen to his inspirational homilies.

The Republicans dismissed General Scott as a coward, despite Grant's praise for him during the Civil War. One of Scott's gaffes, "That the tariff is a local issue," evoked loud guffaws.

The Democrats tried in vain to exploit the corruption issue; Garfield had been linked to the Credit Mobilier receiving $329 from the corrupt holding company and his vice president Arthur's role as a notorious spoilsman. Garfield insisted his was not a bribe but a loan which he later paid off. According to Herbert J. Clancy in a magazine article, "The Presidential Election of 1880," the sum '$329,' scrawled on walls and fences and outhouses "helped pioneer the art of political graffiti. An unusual cartoon ribbon shows Hancock and English on a Cuyahoga River can barge being low-bridged by a wooden span decorated with '329.'

In the final analysis, the return of prosperity after the depression of 1873-79 helped Garfield, as did his party's superb organization and a fat campaign chest.

The Republican duo prevailed with an impressive 214 to 155 electoral romp; Garfield's popular vote margin was closer, 4,454,416 to Scott's 4,444,952, only a 10,000 vote differential. Weaver, the Greenback-Laborite, picked up 308,578.

Garfield's term lasted only four months; on 19 September, 1881, he was assassinated by Charles Gauiteau, a disappointed office-seeker. Ironically, Garfield's successor, the 21st president, Chester A. Arthur, filled in commendably. His administration stands up as the best GOP reign between Lincoln and Theodore Roosevelt. Garfield's campaign fund topped $1 million, the first to go over that magic mark, mere chump change compared to George W. Bush's $200 million war chest in 2004.

Arthur had the courage to veto a Chinese exclusion bill and a river and harbor bill—a monument of pork barreling and even championed civil-service reform. GOP stalwarts felt betrayed and reformers were distrustful of Arthur; he was passed by as the choice to succeed himself.

Collector's Choice

A practical campaign memento in the days of the detachable collar in men's wardrobes comprised a series of four 1880 wooden collar boxes with gutta-percha covers with molded likenesses of Garfield, Arthur, Hancock and English. A Garfield bas-relief milk-glass shaving mug with attached brush holder rates as one of the truly inspired 3-D objects. The Victorian middle-classes' insatiable appetite for decorative bric-a-brac was further sated by a Hancock gem, an effigy tobacco clay pipe with glazed mustard-colored design and rebus of figural hand with rooster (as in Hand Cock) carved along the top of the shank. The Democratic rooster strutting his stuff and wearing an oversized saber rates as one of the classic Hancock gilt brass shellbacks. A whimsical Garfield tin mechanical tin "nose thumber" dangling from a lapel pin is another keeper. Collectors are forever intrigued by a red "Century" tobacco tin with revolving disc in the center of the lid that revolves to picture either Hancock or Garfield.

25th Election—1884

President: Grover Cleveland
Vice President: Thomas Hendricks
Defeated candidates:
James G. Blaine (R) and John Logan
Belva Lockwood (NER)
Benjamin Butler (P) John St. John (PR)

Governor Grover Cleveland of New York limited his campaigning to a few brief speeches urging civil service reform, preferring to continue his duties at the governor's office in Albany. To appease the old guard, Thomas Hendricks of Indiana had been chosen for the vice-presidential slot.

Meanwhile, James Blaine, his GOP opponent, the "Plumed Knight" (dedicated followers were referred to as "Blainiacs"), a popular U.S. senator from Maine crisscrossed the country, delivering over 400 speeches praising Protectionism. Lewis Gould in *Grand Old Party* writes, "No politician of the Gilded Age was better at articulating Republican doctrine and making its appeal to the voters."

Blaine, however, had a cross to bear, having corruptly profited to the tune of $100,000, from his political position as broker for a subsequently bankrupt Little Rock and Fort Smith Railroad. Blaine was exonerated, at first, following a Government investigation of the affair, but the Democrats dredged up the so-called "Mulligan Letters," damaging evidence which exposed him as accepting a bribe for killing a bill that would have deprived the Arkansas railroad of a federal grant.

The Republican's choice for second place, John A. "Black Jack" Logan of Illinois, a Union General and founder of the Grand Army of the Republic (GAR) in 1866, was immensely popular in veteran's circles. Logan, like Blaine, was suspected of crooked railroad dealings and numerous Reformers bolted the party.

Grover Cleveland had dirty linen of his own. Word leaked out that he had paid a substitute to shoulder a musket for him in the Civil War. Pompous, cranky and of generous bulk, Cleveland was known as "Uncle Jumbo" to his nieces and nephews. Democrats were taken aback when Cleveland admitted having sired a bastard child to a Buffalo widow, Bunny Halpin, prompting the ditty "Ma Ma Where's My Pa?" The Democrats after their win in November rejoined "Gone to the White House. Ha! Ha! Ha!"

The Democrats chant of "Blaine! Blaine! Continental liar from the state of Maine" public integrity issue, cost Blaine more dearly than Cleveland's private moral indiscretions. Cleveland triumphed with 219 electoral votes to Blaine's 182 but narrowly squeaked by in the popular count, 4,874,985 to 4,851,981.

The Democrat's win ended 24 frustrating years of Republican dominance—a dry spell harking back to Lincoln's ascension to high office in 1860.

Greenback Ben Butler received 175,370 votes, Prohibitionist John P. John, 150,370 and Belva Lockwood of the Equal Rights party, the first woman to run for the presidency, managed only 4,149.

A 48-year-old bachelor, Cleveland's image soon greatly improved when upon entering the White House, he wooed and married Frances Folsom, a lovely debutante half his age.

Collector's Choice

The 1884 race marked the largest outpouring of campaign objects in the long history of the Democratic Party up to that time with over 200 documented examples, regrettably as dull as the nominee himself. Prized lapel devices incuded a figural train engine, "White House/ Cleveland 1884" with bust portrait; an embossed Courage/Consistency"pin; a figural train engine shellback dated "White House/Cleveland 1884" with bust portrait; a beribboned brass shield pin with profile busts of Cleveland and matching brass circular disc pins portraying Cleveland and wife Francis.

A rather bizarre Butler bisque china matchbox with a Civil War Union cap or kepi on the lid depicts ghostly-pale high relief Butler faces, not unlike death masks. The matchbox cover is inscribed, "Contraband of War/Set Them to Work" and "A Match For Anyone." The term contrabands was coined by Butler when asked how to treat slaves living in Union-occupied territory; from that time on, freed slaves were so categorized.

26th Election—1888

President: Benjamin Harrison (R)
Vice President: Levi Morton
Defeated candidates:
Grover Cleveland (D) and Alan Thurmon
Clinton B. Fisk (PR)
A. J. Streeter (LP)
Belva Lockwood (NER)

Republicans, who for the first time were identified as the Grand Old Party (GOP), convened in Chicago to nominate as their standard-bearer, Benjamin Harrison, a Union general who had distinguished himself leading infantry charges with the 70th Indiana Volunteers. A senator from Indiana and grandson of William Henry Harrison, "Little Ben" was an avowed protectionist, as was his running mate, Levi Morton, a wealthy New York banker.

Incumbent president Grover Cleveland added former Ohio senator Allan Thurman to the slate and took a strong stand on tariff revision.

The Democratic campaign was lackluster at best. Cleveland held the traditional view that it was unseemly that an incumbent lower himself to pander for votes, and refused to budge from the White House. Doddering, Allen Thurman bore the brunt of the campaigning. The 75-year-old did his best to advance the Democrat's advocacy of moderate reductions of tariff duties, not free trade. Thurman, fragile, and well on in years, was known to digress over personal ailments, and on one occasion, collapsed on the platform in mid-speech.

Harrison, too, did very little barnstorming, but conducted an effective front porch campaign in his hometown of Indianapolis, receiving thousands of visitors. The GOP raised over $3 million, the largest campaign coffers to date—primarily from well-heeled industrialists who stood to benefit from high duties on foreign imports.

Harrison topped Cleveland in the Electoral College by 233 to 168, yet pulled almost 100,000 fewer popular votes, 5,044,337 to the Democrats' 5,540,309. Clinton Fisk of the Prohibition Party and Alson Streeter, a Union Laborite, made little headway with 249,506 and 146,935 respectively.

Not since the smoke and mirrors "Old Tippecanoe" campaign of his grandfather William Henry Harrison in 1844, did a candidate so successfully undergo an image makeover—a transformation sorely called for, as little Ben was so void of warmth and good humor, he was nicknamed "the human iceberg."

Collector's Choice

More than 700 varieties of campaign mementos, arguably the most prolific in history, extolled the virtues of

President Benjamin Harrison, more than half of which comprise textiles, primary ribbons and bandanas (see sidebar.) It was 1840 redux, rife with log cabin and cider barrel symbolism. Lapel devices included a white metal figural log cabin fob with raccoon on roof; a brass mechanical badge with Harrison's portrait popping up out of the "Presidential Chair" and " Crowing Rooster" with "Harrison-Morton" jugate brass shell also had a Cleveland-Thurman match.

An eagle with olive branch, arrows in talons gilt brass mechanical; small brass spring activates wings revealing Harrison-Morton ambros.

"Harrison Morton" 1888 white jugate badge of Eagle atop oblong frame has a circular cardboard ambro portraits; tinted; stars and names above busts; r, w, b scroll.

A horseshoe hanger in gilt brass with Harrison-Morton ambros; draped flags; r, w, b; Harrison-Morton images; $3^1/_2$ in. overall.

The 1888 race brought a fascinating flurry of silk and cotton campaign bandannas. Cleveland's running mate, Senator Alan Thurman, was hailed as the "Knight of the Red Bandanna," because of his habit as an ardent snuff dipper, of pulling out a red kerchief from his hip pocket to sneeze into.

Of the several hundreds of designs issued, typically most are of a vibrant Turkey red color, with floral or geometric patterns and candidates' portraits. The patterns of squares on Cleveland-Thurman bandanas became the symbol of consumer rights.

Slogans included: "Protection to Home Industry"; "Protective Tariffs"; "Rights of Workingmen," (Harrison); and "Tariff Reform," "Free Trade." (Cleveland)

A stunning Harrison & Morton 1888-1892 beauty says it all with a border of stars representing every state of the Union, plus an American Eagle screaming "Protection" for its eaglets nesting precariously like America's infant industries. "Let the eagles scream" countered the defiant Democrats who offered a "clean sweep" of import taxes.

27th Election—1892

President: Grover Cleveland
Vice president: Adlai Stevenson
Defeated candidates:
Benjamin Harrrison (RE) and Whitlaw Reid
James B. Weaver (PR)
John Bidwell (P)

Grover Cleveland, rudely unseated in '88, came storming back in '92, denouncing GOP protectionism as a fraud and championing fiscal conservatism with a special emphasis to the gold standard. "The two candidates," observed Henry Adams, "were singular persons . . . of whom it was the common saying that one had no friends; the other only enemies."

Harrison, whose dour personality soon wore thin, grew unpopular with party leaders. Further distracted by the failing health of his wife (she died shortly before the election) "Little Ben" barely put up a struggle. Both parties agreed that the GOP cause was hurt badly by a divisive Carnegie Steel Company strike in Homestead, Pennsylvania, and the strong-arm manner in which it was put down by armed Pinkerton detectives and national guardsmen in a pitched battle with strikers.

Cleveland's electoral edge was decisive, 277 to 145; the popular vote was closer, 5,556,918 to 5,176,108. Entering the fray for the first time, the Populists' James Baird Weaver, made an impressive showing with 1,041,028 popular votes and 22 votes in the Electoral College. Baird's proposals for currency expansion and higher farm prices found receptive voters in the rural Midwest and the South.

Collector's Choice

The GOP's "Harrison and Reid" stenciled blue and white parade horn; the popular clear glass and milk glass mini-beaver "Same Old Hats" curios were reprised from the 1888 race. For Cleveland–Stevenson, a 5-1/2-inch long showpiece "National Association Democratic Clubs/ 1888" jugate shellbadge with crossed flags and suspended anchor; also a pair of clever figural pins, one of a whisk broom, the other a dust pan with circular portraits of Cleveland.

Grover Cleveland—22nd and 24th President

"Cleveland and Thurman" brass shell pin; figural crowing rooster; names embossed across image; gilt brass with red crown.

"National Association Democratic Clubs, 1888" brass framed circular jugate ambrotype; die-stamped irregularly-shaped shield, draped flags, suspended anchor and ribbon; 6 in. h, impressive centerpiece.

Presidential Chair mechanical shell; ambro portrait of Cleveland pops up from cushion; (match appears for opponent Harrison).

"White House Express/1884" train brass shell with Cleveland image fronting the locomotive.

28th Election—1896

President: William McKinley (R)
Vice president: Garrett Hobart
Defeated candidates:
William Jennings Bryan (DP-P) and Arthur Sewell
James Weaver (P) and James Field (P)
John Palmer (ND)
Joshua Levering (PR)

The 1896 McKinley versus Bryan "Battle of Standards" was pitched on the GOP championing the gold standard and the Democrats for unlimited coinage of silver at a 16-1 ratio of ounces of gold. Rather than splitting the silver forces, the Populists finally decided to back the Democrats. In the liveliest race since the Lincoln-McClellan fray of '64, McKinley's campaign chairman Mark Hanna unleashed over 120 million broadsides, some 275 versions. Young Teddy Roosevelt, then president of the Board of Police Commissioners of NYC, was appalled, "He (Hanna) has advertised McKinley as if he were a patent medicine."

The GOP selected Garrett A. Hobart of New Jersey, a president of several banks and railroads and the Passaic Water company. The Dems picked Arthur Sewell, a wealthy Maine shipbuilder, for second place.

Borrowing a page from Garfield and Harrison, McKinley conducted a front porch campaign in his home town of Canton, Ohio. Over 750,000 faithful, some 300 delegations from 30 states, paid a visit to Canton.

Meanwhile, Bryan, the handsome Nebraskan with the magnetic voice, took to the stump, crisscrossing the country, logging over 18,000 miles by train and delivering more than 600 speeches (sometimes as many as 20 to 30 a day) preaching the gospel of free silver, dramatizing such issues as raising farm prices and regulating the railroads.

A record 14 million voters turned out at the polls. Buoyed by a national revival of business after a long depression, coupled with rising prices, McKinley swept to victory with 271 to 176 electoral votes for the Democrat/Peoples (Populist) Party the popular difference favored the GOP with 7,104,779 to 6,502,925. The sectional cleavage was clear: McKinley carried the industrial north and middle west as well as several states in the far west; Bryan, carried the solid south, and the plains and mountain states.

From the collector's perspective, the 1896 campaign has special significance. It not only popularized the celluloid button, the most desirable of all campaign memorabilia, but ushered in the "Golden Age" (1896–1920) of exciting, imaginative designs combining pictures, slogans and vibrant colors that remain unmatched in quality to this day.

Among buttons reflecting the GOP's key slogan "McKinley and the Full Dinner Pail" and blatant appeal to the workingman, were a number of exciting designs, including a keystone to any McKinley collection, worded "Do You Smoke/Yes Since 1896/That's What McKinley Promises"—imagery that would clearly be a turnoff to environmentalists today.

Collector's Choice

"Canton for Me/Known The World Over City" bowling ball and tenpins, with small McKinley bust inset; Canton was McKinley's home town, where he conducted his front porch campaign in 1900; b, w; 1¹/4 in.

Carnation: "We Will Bloom Again for McKinley" 1900; multicolor; 1¹/4 in.

"Gold Didn't Get There July 7th But Watch Us Take It There Nov. 3" 1896; McKinley-Hobart on tandem bike; teal blue on white; 1¹/4 in.

"My Hobby/A Winner" 1900; cartoon pin McKinley in Napolean-type cocked hat riding hobbyhorse with broom attached; multicolored; $2^1/8$; purportedly issued as an advertising promotion; has a Bryan match.

"To The White House" bicycler McKinley wearing beanie; "Gold" and "Silver" appear on wheels; w, blk, gld trim; $7/8$ in.

McKinley portrait pin flanked by symbols of industry; multicolor; $1^1/4$ in.

"Erie County Rep. Org; McKinley-Hobart," 1896 jugate; r, w, b, blk; $1^1/4$ in.

"McKinley-Roosevelt Musical Notes"; furled banner with musical notes in gold to remind voters of gold standard plank; oval $1^3/4$ in.

McKinley-Roosevelt jugate photos draped with large r, w, m. b ribbon; gold, b, g; $1^1/4$, also found in $7/8$, 2 in. sizes.

"McKinley-Roosevelt" jugate, 1900; images in slanted ovals with elaborate filigree gold surround; blk, w; gld; $1^1/4$ in.

"A Full Dinner Pail" McKinley-Roosevelt jugate with images inside bucket; b, blk, gld; $1^1/4$ in. numerous variations of theme.

"McKinley-Hanna" jugate; '96 nominee paired with his campaign manager, GOP kingpin Mark Hanna; sepia; $4^1/2$ by 6 in. centerpiece.

"McKinley-Hobart Protection Eagle"; 1896 with dollar signs on wings perched on globe of North America; superb multicolor; $1^1/4$ in.

"The Right Men/The Right Place At The Right Time," 1900 mutigate of McKinley-TR; flag insets of Washington, Lincoln, Grant ; g, r, w, b, blk; $1^1/4$ in.

29th Election—1900

President: William McKinley (R)
Vice President: Theodore Roosevelt
Defeated candidates:
William J. Bryan (D) and Adlai Stevenson
Eugene Debs (SD)
Job Harriman (SD of USA))

Wharton Barker (P)
John G. Wooley (PR)

The final presidential campaign in the nineteenth century was anything but a rip-snorter. McKinley's vice-president Garret Hobart, passed away, only two years into the 1896 administration.

Human dynamo Theodore Roosevelt of New York, the illustrious Rough Rider and former NYC police commissioner was the GOP vice presidential choice, despite the objections of king-maker Mark Hanna— appalled that there would be "only one life between this madman and the White House."

Roosevelt's vice presidential counterpart, Adlai Stevenson, a two-term congressman from Illinois, was Cleveland's vice president in 1892; a noted patron of the spoils system. Stevenson in one fell swoop, had phased out 40,000 Republican postmasters and replaced them with Democrats, clearly earned the nickname "The Axeman."

Riding the crest of prosperity that engulfed the nation at the turn of the century, victory was assured for McKinley. The GOP pulled 292 electoral votes to the Democrats 155 and led 7,207,923 to 6,358, 133. John Wooley of the Prohibition Party gained 208,914 votes.

Collector's Choice—William Jennings Bryan-Democratic Nominee—1896, 1900, 1908

A recent discovery in the hobby of a multicolor "Expansion" button showing McKinley and TR preventing Bryan from taking down Old Glory over an outline map of the Philippines, rates at the top of a bumper crop of 1900 gems.

"A Clean Sweep"; Rooster with broom under wing; 1900; multicolor; 7/8 in.

"Clean Sweep for Democracy/Bryan-Kern" jugate; stylized broom separates portraits; b, r, y; 1 1/4 in. key item for 1908 race.

"Anti-Imperialism" inscribed in Latin on rim; seated Liberty holds globe with North American outline; wreath over Bryan's head; multicolor; 1 1/4 in.; "Bryan & Uncle Sam offer constitutional government to Puerto Rico"; large snake labeled "Trusts" coiled to crush crown-wearing McKinley, 1900; sepia; 1 1/4 in.

"Bryan the Full of Trusts Dinner Pail"; Bryan claims his pail contains more than lunch— assets like "Wire, Sugar, Leather, Tobacco, Tin, Oil, Beef, Biscuit"; vibrant red b.g. w, blk; $1^1/4$ in.

Bryan "Money of the Constitution/Silver and Gold at 16-1"; reddish brown, w. $1^1/2$ in.

Bryan Racetrack cartoon, 1906, with Bryan riding donkey in lead; Taft trails in distance; blk, w; $2^1/4$ in. (Taft match.)

"Democracy Stands for Bimetalism Not Nonmetalism/People Not Trusts/Republic Not Empire"; one of many long-winded Bryan pins; words appear in three leaf clover; blk, w, brn; $1^1/4$.

"Enemies of Speech Privilege/Upholders of Equality Above the Law"; multi-gate with Bryan, center, surrounded by Washington, Jefferson, Jackson & Lincoln; multicolor; $1^1/4$ in.

"First, Last and All the Time; Denver/1908/Wm. J. Bryan"; browntone; $3^1/2$ in. Motto also appears on small br, light tan $7/8$ single picture pin.

"My Hobby/A Winner" cartoon pin of Bryan Riding an ostrich-headed broom stick" multicolored; 2 in.

"No Crown of Thorns/No Cross of Gold/Bryan" bust of Bryan; inspired by Bryan's ringing oratory at 1896 convention; gold, blk, cr $1^1/4$ in. another Bryan entry depicts thorn entwining gold Cross w, gld, blk; $7/8$ in.

"Partial Eclipse Will Be Total in November" Bryan image, obscures most of McKinley face; br; w (one of a half dozen variations, also with McKinley match; was inspired by May 28, 1900 solar eclipse.)

"Patriotism/Prosperity/The People Will Not Vote Themselves Into the Poorhouse Twice In Eight Years" shows the Sands of Luzon military cemetery; 1900; r, w, b, blk; 2 in.

"People's Airline" cartoon pin of Bryan balancing on high wire in the clouds, en route to Washington; b, w; $1^1/4$ in.

"Bryan Clock" pin; dial shows time as 16-1; imaginative reference to Free Silver issue; brn, w, r, w, b, rim; $1^1/2$.

1908 William J. Bryan "Twilight Zone" cartoon pin illustrates eternal struggle between federal and states jurisdiction; white, black; 2 in.

"Our Standard Bearer/The Nation's Commoner/William Jennings Bryan/Two Great Essentials Known the World Over" pictures Bryan bust atop shocks of corn; one husk is labeled, "From Mr. Bryan's Fairview farm"; key 1908 item; multicolor; oval 2³/8 by 1⁵/8 in.

"Tree of Life"; "Tree That Does Not Bear Good Fruit Shall Be Dug Out By the Roots and Cast Into the Fire" Bryan's fundamentalist philosophy; square inset of seated flanked by dead tree being dug out and tree that is flourishing; 1908 key item; gr, blk; buff; 1¹/2 in. (also in ⁷/8 in.)

Bryan picture pin; art nouveau design by Maxfield Parish; one design shows Bryan image with Court Herald blowing horn; the other with Miss Liberty on throne; multicolor; 1³/4 in.

"United We Stand/Divided We Fall/No Trusts/16-1"; Bryan shakes hands with bearded figure labeled "Labor"; multicolor; 1¹/4 in.

Cartoon pin depicting Bryan sitting in chair on McKinley's atop prostrate figure; 1896; multicolor; ⁷/8. (McKinley Match with positions reversed.)

Anti-Bryan
"Imaginary Eclipse/Visible Only at Kansas City, July 4"; refers to Democratic convention in that city; large bust of McKinley with tiny inset of Bryan; y, blk, buff; 1¹/4.

"In God We Trust, for the Other 47 cents" caricature of Bryan; b, w; ⁷/8 in.

Soup Kettle cartoon pin with Bryan's head popping out of it; blk, w; 1¹/4 in.

30th Election—1904
President: Theodore Roosevelt (R)
Vice president: Charles W. Fairbanks
Defeated candidates:
Alton B. Parker (D) and Henry Davis
Silas Swallow (PR)

After McKinley's assassination on September 6, 1901 Theodore Roosevelt filled out the last three years of his term as president. Roosevelt became increasingly agitated by snide references to "His Accidency" upon becoming the 26th president.

Charles W. Fairbanks, an Old Guard conservative senator from Indiana, was chosen as Roosevelt's number two. Although he proved a good balance for the president, his attempt to thwart Roosevelt's Square Deal reform program and his blatant presidential ambitions* created a rift between the two. Fairbanks acted in revenge by working to defeat TR and his Bull Moosers in 1916.

TR's "Square Deal" embracing conservation of national resources, regulation of big corporations in the public interest, and friendliness to labor, drew widespread support.

TR's opponent, conservative Judge Alton Parker of New York, Chief Justice of the New York Court of Appeals, was a supporter of the gold standard. He spent most of his time in seclusion at his Ulster County, New York home, an example followed by most of his supporters including running mate, Henry G. Davis, an 82-year-old millionaire, little known out of his home state of West Virginia.

Roosevelt after also waging a surprisingly passive campaign, won by a landslide. It marked the biggest disparity in electoral votes since Jackson trounced Clay in 1832, winning 336 electoral votes to the Democrats 140. TR won 7,628,785 popular votes (57.4 percent) to Parker's 5,084,442. TR gleefully told his wife, "I am no longer a political accident." During his second term Roosevelt sponsored stricter railroad regulation, more conservation measures, and a Pure Food and Drug Act. There was no shortage of Democratic campaign devices—inspiring as many as a thousand different buttons, nearly a hundred varieties of watch fobs, numerous posters, ribbons and postcards, paperweights and ceramic plates.

---

*Humorist Finely Peter Dunne once advised TR not to take a planned submarine trip "unless you take Fairbanks with you."

TR forces again trotted out items exploiting his fame as the hero of San Juan Hill in the War of 1898. Surprisingly, TR objects in 1904 were remarkably devoid of militaristic calls to national glory that dominated so many 1900 McKinley relics.

Collector's Choice—Alton Parker, Democratic Nominee, 1904

Capitol dome outlined against flag, stars and stripes frame Parker portrait; r, w, b, flesh tones; $1^1/4$ in.

"Hoeing His Way To The White House" cartoon pin of Parker as farmer plowing in fields; "For President/Alton B. Parker"; multicolor; $1^1/2$ in.

"Judge We're It" Parker-Roosevelt busts on Fairbanks scales weighed by Uncle Sam; has Rooster looking on and scales tilted in Parker's favor; multicolor; $1^1/2$ in. (TR match.)

"Parker-Davis" jugate in Liberty Cap, 1904; r, w, b, blk, gold; $1^1/4$. (Has TR mate.)

"Parker-Davis" circular bust insets with jugate crossed flags with scepter; r, w, b, blk, bronze b, g; $1^1/2$ in.

"Parker-Davis" key jugate; sunburst with eagle and pair of U.S. flags; sepiatone; $2^1/4$ in.

Alton Parker "Star" pin; 1904; Parker bust in side large Tammany star with six furled U.S. flags: multicolor; $1^1/4$ in.

"Shure Mike" Parker-Davis jugate; photos flank large Rooster in stars and stripes costume; multicolor; $1^1/4$ in.

"Uncle Sam's White Elephant/It's Game/It's Finishes" elephant astride giant football with banner labeled "Protection," elephant blanket reads: "Grand Old Pirate" 1904 classic; r, br, w, blk; $1^1/2$ in.

"Wedding Cake," "It's Up To You/Take Your Choice" venal image of Parker and TR hovering over wedding scenes; Parker's shows handsome Caucasian bride and groom; TR—black groom in top hat and white bride; sepiatone; $1^1/4$ in.

"We Will Chop Our Way to the White House in 1904" crossed flags under inset image of Jefferson "Father of Democracy;" pierced hole has small hatchet attachment.

Collector's Choice—26th President Theodore Roosevelt

"A Square Deal" TR picture pin with one of the most memorable of campaign slogans; b, w; 1¹/4 in.

"De-light-ed" surreal cartoon word-play with light bulbs representing TR's eyes; emphasizes famed prominent teeth; promotes virtues of electricity as new home-lighting system. White reversed out of black; ⁷/8 in.

"Equality-Protection" TR stands in middle as mediator between top hatted and blue-color figures denoting capital and labor; r, w, b, g, blk; 1¹/4 in.

"Four More Years with Theodore" 1900; top-hatted TR and running mate Fairbanks stroll hand in hand as teddy bear follows; Clifford Berryman cartoon; b, w; 1¹/4 in.

"Isthmian Canal at Panama" overhead view showing projected Canal route from Pacific to Atlantic; play on word veldt (Dutch for lush fields); sea green, buff, black, rose; 1¹/4 in.

"Join the Bandwagon" cartoon pin of elephant beating drum with TR's image inside drum; multicolor; 1¹/4 in.

"National Unity/Republican Party/Prosperity/Advancement" TR flanked by U.S. flags; multicolor; 1¹/4 in.

"Let Well Enough Alone" TR-Fairbanks jugate; portraits appear inside eye-glass design on lunch pail; extols the full-lunch pail prosperity theme advanced by McKinley in

1896; dark brown, white; $1^1/_4$ in; also known in a black variant.

"Our Teddy Never Pulls Leather" 1904 cartoon pin of T.R. riding bucking bronco; sepiatone; $1^1/_4$ in.

"Roosevelt-Fairbanks" jugate stunner with oval images inside pair of large furled flags; r, w, b, blk; $1^1/_4$ in.

"Roosevelt-Parker" 1900 cartoon classic; two fighting cocks locked in battle with feathers flying; b, w; $1^1/_4$ in.

"T.R. at the Gate" Equality classic; TR stands at gate with Uncle Sam, raises first banner labeled "Prejudice" above sunburst at top; "The Spirit of the Republic-Success 1904/President to All The People" appears on path to Capitol; multicolor; key item epitomizing pro-equality theme; multicolor; $1^1/_2$ in.

"Stand Pat" Hand" holding five cards, four aces and a TR card; r, w, blk; 1 in., rarest of several sizes.

A few other TR pins with the poker hand theme include two unlisted beauties: "The People's Choice/A Square Deal and Straight Hand" shows five cards fanned out over TR's portrait; multicolor; $1^1/_2$ in.

"Republicans Must Elect a President and Coattail Congress" another variant—a trigate showing card-player's hand holding three cards; pictures TR, Fairbanks and Henry B. Cassell, Pennsylvanian running for congress; w, blk; $1^1/_4$ in.

"You Can't Beat It/TR" is pictured as the Ace of diamonds in a Royal Flush with cards worded "Protection, Prosperity, Expansion" above cards; multi; $1^1/_4$ in.

T.R.-Booker T. Washington no-name "Equality" pin; Pair dining at White House, October 1901; multicolor version; $1^1/_4$ in. at least four variants exist.

Africa Return—1910

Although not campaign-related per se, a spectacular array of buttons signaled TR's return from African safari to the political arena, setting the stage for his 1912 run.

"Buano Tumbo" (Swahili for great master); bust portrait appears above inscription; b, w; $1^1/_4$ in. Uncle Sam Embraces T.R.

"Welcome" single word above head of TR as rising sun; Uncle Sam tips hat to him in b g; multicolor; $1^1/4$ in.

"Welcome From Elba" Jubilant Uncle Sam TR on return from Africa; just off the boat and still in Safari regalia; multicolor; $1^3/4$ in.

"Good Scales Teddy"; classic cartoon pin; GOP elephant with images of TR and Parker on Fairbanks scale being weighed by Uncle Sam; tips in Roosevelt's favor; multicolor; $1^1/2$ in.

TR Saluting on Horseback; in Rough Rider uniform; 1904; multicolor; $1^1/4$ in.

31st Election—1908

President: William Howard Taft (R)
Vice President: James S. Sherman
Defeated candidates:
William Jennings Bryan (D) and John W. Kern
Thomas Watson (P) Eugene Debbs and Ben Hanford

Theodore Roosevelt declined to run again in 1908, but there was little doubt that he had masterfully pulled the strings for his secretary of war William Howard Taft of Ohio as his hand-picked choice. One of the campaign jokes was that T-A-F-T spelled "Take Advice From Theodore." Taft's choice for vice president was James "Sunny Jim" Sherman of Utica, an affluent New York businessman and a twenty-year U.S. congressman. Early in the Taft presidency, Sherman's differences over reform programs were to cause a major rift. Later, Roosevelt, convinced that Taft had sold out to the Old Guard, also had a parting of the ways and set the stage for a direct confrontation between the two in 1912.

The Democrat's vice-presidential counterpart, John W. Kern of Indiana, was a spellbinding speaker who enjoyed great popularity in the West.

Bryan in his third try for the presidency resurrected an old theme from campaigns past—a choice between a government devoted to people's rights and government by privilege. Taft countered that Bryan's views were "full

of sophistries" and would paralyze business.

Taft became the 27th president by winning a popular majority of over a million at 7,104,779 to 6,502,925 and topped the Great Commoner 321 to 162 in electoral votes—the worst of Bryan's three defeats. John G. Wooley of the Prohibition Party placed third at 208,914 and Socialist Eugene Debs, running for third time, polled 87,814.

Collector's Choice—27th President William Howard Taft

GOP elephant with tiny Taft–Sherman jugate insets; 1912; browntone, cream; 7/8 in.

"I Am a Tafty Kid" cartoon pin; Taft wears beanie, looking even heftier than usual; r, w, b, blk; 1 7/8 in.

"Liberty Halo" jugate; Taft–Sherman portrait insets in folds of Liberty's red striped skirt; multicolor; 1 in.

"Possum Klub" (sic) image of possum on tree limb; sepiatone; 1 1/4 in.

"Race Track" Taft rides elephant and outraces Bryan on donkey, lagging far behind; b, w; 2 in. Bryan mate.

Steamroller cartoon pin 1908; Taft portrait oval above steamroller; b, w; 1 1/4 in.

"Taft/From Chicago To Washington" cartoon of Taft astride Elephant wielding big club; r, w, blk; 1 1/4 in.

"Taft–Sherman/Bloomington, Illinois" portraits with ear of corn; y, g, b, w, blk; 1 1/4 in.

"Taft and Sherman" jugate; dynamic photos with stars and stripes b g: r, w, b, blk 2 1/8 in.

"Taft-Sherman Lady Liberty" no-name jugate; portraits appear atop each other next to seated Liberty with elaborate laurel wreath and flag sur-round; multicolor; 1³/4 in.

"The Winners" Taft-Sherman ju-gate with stars, scepter; made by American Artworks, Coshocton, Ohio; multicolor; 1¹/4 in.

"The Butting Bills/Which One Will Win" pair of goats locking horns referring to Bill Taft and Bill Bryan.

Anti-Taft

"What Is a Man to Do When Out of Work In a Financial Crisis and Starving? God Knows!" caricature of obviously well-fed 350-pound Taft looking perplexed; b, w; 1¹/4 in.

1908 William H. Taft–James Sherman "Statue of Liberty" 1¹/₄ in. multicolor jugate (31st election).

32ⁿᵈ Election—1912

President: Woodrow Wilson (D)
Vice President: Thomas Marshall
Defeated candidates:
William Howard Taft (R)
and James Sherman
Theodore Roosevelt (PG) and Hiram Johnson
Eugene Debs (S) and Emil Seidel
Eugene Chafin (PR)

A spellbinding three-cornered race kept the populace on the edge of their seats throughout the countdown to the 1912 election. The GOP was split as the regulars renomi-nated the incumbent, the genial but aroused William H. Taft. The insurgents, called the Progressives or Bull Moosers, were led by the mercurial TR who stormed out of the GOP convention in Chicago after Taft was nominated to run for a second term. This, despite the fact that TR had bested him in nine primaries to one, including Ohio, Taft's home state. The Democrat's standard bearer was New Jersey Governor Woodrow Wilson, a liberal and an intel-lectual with a Ph.D. from Johns Hopkins University.

All three candidates recognized that a "new day" had dawned for America, laissez-faire no longer seemed ade-quate, and it was the duty or government to concern it-self with general welfare.

The vice-presidential nominees were Governor Thomas Marshall of Indiana for the Democrats; the GOP again tapped James S. Sherman but when he died on October

30, Columbia University president Nicolas Murray Butler replaced him on the ticket; for the Bull Moosers, TR's running mate was Senator Hiram Johnson of California.

TR's "New Nationalism" program called for regulation of big business in the national interest. Wilson took it a step further in his "New Freedom" platform, calling for breaking up the monopolies and restoring freedom of competition.

Wilson, in becoming the 28th president, gained only 41.9 percent of the popular vote, less than Bryan had won in each of his three ties, and it was evident that he gained immeasurably from the split in the GOP ranks to win election. Wilson's victory in the electoral college proved decisive as he carried 40 of the 48 states, with 435 votes to TR's 88 and Taft's meager 8. The popular vote was Wilson: 6,293,454; Roosevelt: 4,119,538; Taft: 3,484,980. Socialist Eugene Debs, creeping ever upward, won 900,672 votes.

The Progressives in 1912 were woefully short of campaign funds. TR would later lament "There were no loaves and no fishes." The Bull Moosers in campaign mementos, made up for a lack of working capital with imagination and bravado. The prominent teeth, his pince-nez spectacles and gleeful expression, "Dee-lighted" were used freely to create highly innovative caricature buttons; the ubiquitous Moose became a dominant party symbol, clearly upstaging the GOP elephant and Democratic donkey.

33rd Election—1916

President: Woodrow Wilson (D)
Vice President: Thomas Marshall
Defeated candidates:
Charles E. Hughes (R)and Charles Fairbanks
Allen L. Benson (S)
James Franklin Hanly (P)
Theodore Roosevelt (PG)

The dominant campaign issue was preserving neutrality in the wake of a raging conflict that erupted in Europe in

1914. Wilson forces adoped one of the most memorable slogans in campaign history, "He Kept Us Out of War."

The GOP chose Supreme Court Justice Charles Evans Hughes, a former governor of New York, and moderate progressive Charles Fairbanks, TR's sidekick in 1904.

Hughes often vacillated on issues, sometimes accusing Wilson of not taking a hard line with Germany, at other times favoring a strict neutrality. Meanwhile, TR attacked Wilson as "a damned Presbyterian hypocrite" and his hawkish pronouncements in Hughes's behalf proved to be the Justice's albatross. Some observers attributed Hughes's narrow defeat to his having avoided Californian Hiram Johnson (TR's running mate in 1912) on his Western tour and failed to enlist Johnson's support.

The election was so close and Hughes had picked up such overwhelming support on the eve of the election from the Eastern bloc that the *New York Times* and the *New York World* conceded the GOP the election. When all the returns filtered in at week's end, Wilson had swept the entire west, as well as the solid south. Final tally: Wilson 277 electoral votes to Hughes' 254; The popular vote was 9,129,606 to 8,538,221; Socialist Louis Benson was third at 585,113; while Teddy Roosevelt won a small smattering of 35,034 votes. One month after Wilson took his oath of office, the United States declared War on Germany.

Woodrow Wilson had the distinction of holding the first Presidential press conference on March 15, 1913, just 11 days after his first inauguration; some 125 newsmen attended.

Wilson received the Nobel Peace Prize in 1919. Theodore Roosevelt in 1906 and Jimmy Carter in 2002 are the other presidential recipients.

Collector's Choice
28th President Woodrow Wilson
"For President Woodrow Wilson/James M. Cox for Governor" 1916 jugate and outstanding coattail with silk "Reception" ribbon; w, br, blk; $1^1/_2$ in.

"I Stand with President Wilson Against Lynching" slogan pin; r, w, blk; $^7/_8$ in.

"I've Paid My $1/Have You?" Wilson-Marshall jugate in bluetone; white reverse lettering in deep blue b g; 1^1/4 in.

"I Would Row Wilson and Marshall To Victory/Win With Wilson" 1912 classic rebus; pair is being rowed in small skiff on the Potomac with Capitol Building in b g; multicolored; 1^1/4 in.

"League of Nations" Wilson photo flanked by flags of world nations pin; vibrant multicolor; 1^1/4 in.

"Wilson 8-Hour Club" 1916 picture pin with photo and words in stylized figure 8; stresses 8-hour workday; b, gld, w, blk; oval 1^7/16 x 1^1/16.

"Wilson-Pershing" 1918 diamond-shaped jugate; Wilson with Gen. John Pershing chief of AEF in World War II; r, w, b, blk; 1^1/4;

"Wilson Welcomes the US, Navy/Flags Photo Montevideo; Wilson single picture; sepiatone; ^{7}/8 in.

"Winners" 1912 Wilson-Marshall jugate with names on red scroll,w, b, blk, gold scepter b g; mate to Taft "winners."

Charles Evans Hughes, GOP Nominee, 1916

"For President/Charles E. Hughes" scarce single picture pin; blk bust on decal edge buff with red border; 1^1/4 in.

"Hughes" slogan button with the U and S enlarged and highlighted in red; r, w, b; ^{7}/8.

"Hughes" single picture button flanked by US flags; Hughes picture buttons rarely surface and most are in drab b, w; this one's an exception; r, w, b, blk gld; 1^1/4 in.

"Hughes," only bearded nominee in the twentieth century, wears an Uncle Sam hat; a die-cut button hanger; w, blk; 1^1/4

"Hughes Democracy" half-profile single picture button; cr, blk; ^{7}/8 in.

"Hughes and Direct Nominations" slogan button; Hughes' plea to persuade Progressives to return to GOP fold in 1916; entailed direct nomination of candidates; r, w; oval 2^1/2 by 1^1/4 in.

"Hughes and Fairbanks" cartoon name button; 1916 appears on blanket of Elephant; b, w; 1^1/4 in.

"Hughes-Fairbanks" 1916 jugate; sepiatone in brass frame; ribbon r, w, b with silver lettering; 1³/4 in. button; 3¹/8 by 1⁵/8 in. ribbon.

Hughes-Fairbanks no-name jugate, which spelled the end of the Golden Era of buttons; furled flag links ovals; multicolor; 1¹/4 in.

Hughes "Notification Meeting" pre-presidential picture button; when nominated for Governor of New York in 1908; r, w, b gld, blk; 1³/4 in.

Alliterative Calvin Coolidge pin from 1924 (35th Election).

34ᵗʰ Election—1920

President: Warren G. Harding (R)
Vice President: Calvin Coolidge
Defeated candidates:
James D. Cox (D) and Franklin D. Roosevelt
Eugene Debs (S) and Seymour Stedman

Two Ohioans—Republican Warren Harding, a senator and publisher of the *Marion Star and Democrat,* and James Cox, a mildly progressive governor and an editor of the *Cincinnati Inquirer* squared off for the 1920 presidency. (But for his disability, Wilson, who suffered a stroke in his second term, clearly would have received the Democrat's nod.)

The choice in 1920, said the *Nation*, "was between Debs and Dubs." Debs, of course, was Eugene Victor Debs, the Socialist front-runner, running for president from an Atlanta penitentiary where the Wilson administration had put him on sedition charges for anti-war speeches during World War I.

Former Massachusetts Governor Calvin Coolidge was picked as Harding's vice president. His fame rested on having broken a police strike in Boston in 1919. Cox's running mate, Franklin D. Roosevelt, served as Wilson's Assistant Secretary of the Navy. The future 29th president Harding, whose chief contribution to the campaign was the slogan "Back to Normalcy" was content to conduct a front-porch campaign back in Marion (Ohio).

Cox, meanwhile, indulged in some legitimate campaigning, traveled 22,000 miles and spoke to two million people in a valiant effort to whip up support for Wilson's league. *The Literary Digest,* which sent out millions of postcards in what was the first definitive poll ever conducted during a presidential campaign, correctly predicted an overwhelming GOP victory. Harding won 60.2 percent of the popular votes: 16,152,200 to Cox's 9,147,353, a plurality of 7,004,847, breaking all records. Harding's electoral edge was also lopsided: 404 votes to Cox's 127. Debs at 919,799.

Collector's Choice
29th President Warren G. Harding

"Best Ever"; Harding picture pin with cartoon of elephant heads, shield; advertising tie-in with Schoenberg Bros. Clothes makers, Chicago; also known in Cox example; r, w, b, blk; 1³/₄ in.

"Harding For President" picture pin of a rarely smiling Harding; b w; 1¹/₄

"Souvenir President Harding's Pacific Coast Tour" Harding bust with draped US flags; Harding fell ill on tour, suffered fatal heart attack in San Francisco, making this button doubly significant; r, w, b, blk; 1¹/₄ in.

"For President/Harding—For Vice-President/Coolidge" 1920 jugate; names in ornate scrollwork; sepiatone; ⁷/₈ in.

"Harding For Governor" marks Harding's 1910 bid for Ohio Governor, a race he lost to Judson Harmon; r, w; ⁵/₈ in.

Collector's Choice
James M. Cox-Democratic Nominee 1920

Any of the dozen known Cox-Roosevelt jugate varieties are exalted in the hobby, ranking in ultimate scarcity, alongside the 1924 John-Davis-Charles Bryan and 1912 TR-Johnson pairings.

The Cox-FDR button that gets all the notoriety, an Hake unlisted 1¹/₄ inch with conjoining bust images, set the world record of $33,000 at the celebrated 1981 Don Warner Auction. Generally overlooked is an equally stunning Cox-Roosevelt sold a few minutes later at the Warner session to publisher Malcolm Forbes Jr., the underbidder to labor lawyer Joe Jacobs in the first Cox-

Roosevelt blockbuster lot. The second jugate sold for exactly one-tenth that of its predecessor.

"Cox" raised-dome design single portait pin against stars in blue field at top; strips flank circle and below; r, w, b, blk; $1^3/_4$ in. Previously unknown until 1982.

"Cox And Cocktails"; slogan pin, white out of black; $7/_8$ in.

"James M. Cox" photo pin; sepiatone; $1^3/_4$ in.

"Cox-Roosevelt" jugate; known as the St. Louis (mfgr.) button; w, blk; $7/_8$ in. also known in $1^1/_4$ in.

Cox-Roosevelt "Americanize America" construed to have extreme rightist Ku Klux Klan overtones; r, w, b; $7/_8$ in.

"Cox Sure" FDR, Cox's running mate, despised this slogan; dark and light blue; 1 /2 in.

"Crow/Don't Croak" Rooster cartoon; r, w; $7/_8$ in.

"For President/James M. Cox" single picture; fanned r, w, b, stripes flank image; popular centerpiece item at 6 in.

"James M. Cox for President" Cox portrait centered on flank of cartoon bucking donkey; b, w, blk; $1^1/_4$ in.

35th Election—1924

President: Calvin Coolidge (R)
Vice President: Charles Dawes
Defeated candidates:
John Davis (D) and Charles Bryan
Robert LaFollette (PG) and Burton Wheeler
William Z. Foster (C)

Calvin Coolidge was sworn in as the 30th US president, when Harding died of a heart attack in August 1923 and the electorate decided to send Silent Cal back to Washington in 1924.

Coolidge emerged unscathed by the shocking revelations of the Teapot Dome scandals that implicated many of Harding's high ranking aides. Corruption and bribery, however, became a pivotal issue. John Davis, another Ohioan and a Wall Street lawyer along with progressive "Fightin'" Bob LaFollette from Wisconsin, put Coolidge on the defensive, but the stoic Vermonter; lived up to his slogan "Keep Cool with Coolidge."

When GOP leaders asked Coolidge to suggest a running mate, he said he would let the convention pick for him.

"It did in 1920," he added, "and it picked a darn good man." Former budget director Charles G. Dawes of Chicago, known as "Hell an'Maria" for his rampaging platform style, and who had never before held elective office, joined Coolidge on the slate. Charles Bryan, William Jennings Bryan's low-profile brother, was picked as the Democratic vice-presidential candidate in the hope of dispelling the Wall Street curse.

Despite the buzz over the Teapot Dome, to millions, Coolidge meant continued prosperity and the result was another GOP landslide. Coolidge polled 382 electoral votes to 136 for Davis and eight for LaFollette. Coolidge's popular total of 15,725,016 exceeded that of Davis (8,386,503) and LaFollette (4,822,856) combined. Although Fightin' Bob topped TR's 1912 total, he carried only his home state of Wisconsin.

The radio was being used to reach the masses for the first time, undoubtedly contributing to fewer campaign buttons and other promotional items."

Collector's Choice
30th President Calvin Coolidge

"Coolidge–Dawes" jugate; sepiatone; 1 1/4 in.

"Coolidge–Dawes" "Full (rebus) Dinner Pail"; reprieves McKinley's 1896 prosperity theme; r, w, b; 7/8 in.

"Coolidge & Dawes for the Nation's Cause" shield tops jugate insets; r, w, blk; 1 1/4 in.

"Coolidge Fourth of July Club" illustration of Liberty Bell; r, w, b, gld; 7/8 in.

"Courage/Confidence and Coolidge" slogan button; r, w, blk; 3/4 in.

Coolidge no-name Keystone single picture button Pennsylvania (Keystone State) issue; b, w, blk; 7/8 in.

"Coolidge/Dawes Lincoln Tour" outline map of US tracing campaign route; r, w, b; 7/8 in.

"Home Town Coolidge" portrait pin; r, b gr, w; 7/8 in.

"Keep Cool With Coolidge" slogan pin; w, blk; 7/8 in.

"Keep Coolidge For President" circle Coolidge portrait "Firm as the Rock Of Ages"; r, w, b, blk; 7/8 in.

"Keep Square Deal/Coolidge" words in square panel surrounding single picture of Coolidge; w, blk; 5/8 in.

"On the Square" illustration of red schoolhouse; r, w, b; 7/8 in.

"Our Candidates/Coolidge-Dawes" jugate with sunburst; 6 in. w/wire easel.

Items from the 1924 Davis-Bryan campaign remain the most elusive of the button era. The original Davis project initiated by the American Political Items Collectors cataloged just 33 items. Today as more Davis items continue to surface, the number has increased to over 70 including two earlier congressional buttons.

Collector's Choice
John W. Davis

"Back To Honesty with Davis" slogan pin; w, blk; 7/8 in.

"Better Days with Davis" cartoon of teapot slogan pin; b, w; 7/8 in.

Democratic Rooster Crowing cartoon pin 1924; r, w; 5/8 in.

"For President/John W. Davis"; single picture pin; w, brn; 13/4 in.

"For President/Vice-President/J.W. Davis-C.W. Bryan/Honest Government" key integrity theme; white black; 11/4 in; only Davis message jugate; discovered as late as 1982.

"Davis and Bryan" 1924 jugate w, blk; 11/4 in.

"Davis and Bryan-Nebraska" oval w, blk; 11/4 by 3/4 in.

"Davis and Bryan Club/St. Joseph, Mo." jugate, oval pinback; w, blk; 11/4 in. x 3/4 in.

"GOP/Your Waterloo" cartoon of teapot superimposed on Capitol dome; sepiatone; 1/2 in.

"Notification" embossed bar ribbon badge, "John Davis, Aug. 11, 1924/Clarksburg, West Virginia"; embossed log cabin in foreground; skyscrapers in b, g; brass finish; 11/2 in.

"Teapot Dome" 1924 anti-GOP cartoon of elephant sweating inside steaming tea pot; r, w, gray, blk; 1 in.

Al Smith's trademark brown derby frames classic Smith-Robinson jugate; white, brown 4 in. (36th Election).

"Victory"; wishbone-framed single Davis portrait with r, w, b, banner; $7/8$ in.

36th Election—1928

President: Herbert Hoover (R)
Vice President: Charles Curtis
Defeated candidates:
Alfred E. Smith (D)
and Joseph T. Robinson
Norman Thomas (S)
William Z. Foster(C)

When Silent Cal uttered his sphinx-like "I do not choose to run," the GOP turned to Herbert Hoover, a civil engineer, Iowan and former head of the Department of Commerce. Hoover's running mate, Charles Curtis, a Kansas senator and member of the Osage tribe, emerged as the first Native American candidate for high office.

Alfred E. Smith, whose nomination was placed at the Houston convention by FDR as "The Happy Warrior," was a popular four-term governor of New York City and the first Irish Catholic nominee for president. On questions of power regulation, labor and social reform, Smith was progressive; on the touchy prohibition issue, an out-and-out "wet." Senator Joseph G. Robinson of Arkansas balanced the ticket as a Protestant Prohibitionist. One observer quipped that: "The Democratic donkey with a wet head and wagging a dry tail, left Houston." The stage was set for an exciting but down-and-dirty campaign.

Democrats pledged tax revisions and farm relief measures. The GOP called for a continuation of prosperity, but it was Prohibition and the religious issue that figured prominently in giving Hoover a lopsided victory: 58 percent vs. Smith's 41 percent in the popular count, 21,391,381 to 15,016,443; it was a whopping 444 to 87 disparity in the electoral college. Socialist Norman Thomas made little noise at 267,835.

Critic H.L. Mencken summed up the 1928 race: "Those who fear the Pope outnumber those who are tired of the anti-Saloon League."

Collector's Choice
31st President Herbert Hoover

"O.K. America/Play Safe with Hoover" single-picture button; r, w, b, blk: $1^1/4$ in.

"Herbert Hoover-Charles Curtis" 1928 jugate; key Hoover item; photos framed by draped US banners; capitol Dome; r, w, b brown; 4 in.

"Hoo Hoo Hoover" 1928 cartoon button most attractive of several versions with owl; b, w, br; $5/8$ in.

"Hoover-Curtis for All of US" 1932 jugate with eagle atop portraits; r, w, b gld; blk: $1^1/4$; (has FDR match that reads "Roosevelt-Garner For Repeal And Prosperity.")

"My Country Tis of Thee/The Crisis Is Here" 1932 Statue of Liberty Hoover-Curtis jugate with draped flags; r, w, b; $1^3/4$ in.

"WCTU Vote for Hoover" shows large white ribbon; endorsement of Hoover as a pro-Prohibition "Dry" candidate in 1928; Lt. b, w; $5/8$ in.

Collector's Choice
Alfred E. Smith, Democrat, 1928

"Al and Joe Let's Go" canted oval jugate button; w, blk; $1^3/4$ in.

"Downtown Tammany Smith Club/for President"; r, blk; $1/2$ in.

"For President/American Liberty Smith" letters "A" and "L" heavily outlined; Liberty Bell illustration; w, b; $7/8$ key item.

"From the Sidewalks of New York/Al to the White House"; illustration of New York skyline at left; large arrow points to Nation's Capitol at right; w, blk; tin license attachment.

"Happy Warrior" Al Smith's favorite nickname as slogan button; r, b; white border; $7/8$ in.

"Hello Al/Goodbye Cal" cartoon of Democratic rooster; tie-in with 1928 campaign song; w, r, br; $1^3/4$ in.

"May All Your Wet Dreams Come True" Al Smith anti-prohibition slogan button; r, w, b; $7/8$ in.

"National Democratic Convention, Houston Texas, June 26, 1928" cartoon donkey kicks sand on elephant's backside as it sits chained to Teapot Dome; w, blk; $1^1/4$ in.

"No Oil on Al" slogan button with double stars; w, blk; $^7/8$ in.

"Our Choice/Smith and Robinson;" conjoing silhouette jugate portraits; w, blk; $1^1/4$ in.

"Rockland County Al Smith for President Democratic Club; w, blk; $1^1/4$ in.

"To New Heights with Al" cartoon of hot air balloon rising; w, b; $^7/8$ in.

"The Guiding Star of Our Nation" (rebus of blue star); six furled stars behind silhouetted head of Smith; "Alfred E. Smith of New York"; r, w, b, blk; a less scarce red star version is known; $^7/8$ in.

"Up From the Streets" Al Smith portrait; w, blk; $^7/8$ in.

"What's Under Your Hat/ Al Smith for President; illustration of derby; w, blk; $^7/8$ in.

"Smith for President/Robinson for Vice President"; 1928 jugate portraits inside Smith's trademark brown derby; br, w, blk; 4 in.

37th Election—1932

President: Franklin Delano Roosevelt
Vice President: John Nance Garner
Defeated candidates:
Herbert Hoover (R) and Charles Curtis
Norman Thomas (S)
William Z. Foster

In a rare understatement, Herbert Hoover later acknowledged in his *Memoirs*, "General Prosperity had been an ally in 1928; General Depression was a major enemy in 1932."

When the GOP renominated the Hoover-Curtis slate on first ballots, the mood was gloomy, without the usual eulogies and demonstrations. The Democrats in Chicago, sensing they could win if they avoided major boners, chose 50-year-old Franklin D. Roosevelt, two-time governor of New York; Texan John Nance Garner, the popular Speaker of the House, who actually had his eyes on the presidency, settled for vice president. After FDR's nomination, a disappointed Texan sighed, "It's a kangaroo ticket, stronger in the hindquarters than in the front."

Hoover was the last president to write his own speeches. But this time they sounded dreary, especially over the radio, compared with FDR's cheery offerings. FDR made his first presidential radio address on March 12, 1933; The term "Fireside Chat" was later applied to these radio talks. As Robert Rouse writes in the Spring 1986 *Keynoter,* "so ingrained is the term in popular culture that one might think Roosevelt gave fireside chats weekly; in fact, he averaged only two a year prior to World War II."

The Roosevelt-Garner ticket triumphed by over seven million more popular votes, 22,821,857 to 15,761,845 and pulled 472 vs. 59 electoral votes. (A complete reversal of Hoover's rout of Smith in 1928.)

William Allen White wrote that the election represented a "firm desire on the part of the American people to use government as an agency for human welfare."

38th Election—1936

President: Franklin D. Roosevelt
Vice President: John N. Garner
Defeated candidates:
Alfred M. Landon (R) and Frank Knox
Norman Thomas (S)
Earl Browder
William Lemke (U)

In 1936, FDR, as far as millions of Americans were concerned, was in Democratic Chairman Jim Farley's words, "more popular than the New Deal itself."

The GOP, convening in Cleveland, picked Alfred M. Landon, Governor of Kansas, a former Bull Mooser and fiscal conservative. Another Bull Mooser, Col. Frank Knox, publisher of the *Chicago Daily News* and an arch-conservative, was nominated as vice president.

The GOP resorted to scare tactics, including Red-baiting and dragging out the allegation that the Social Security Act, scheduled to go into effect on January 1, 1937, was a giant swindle. There was little that Alf Landon and the GOP could do to stem the tide.

In the landslide of the century, FDR carried every state except Maine and Vermont, his electoral victory—the greatest since Monroe's in 1820—gave him 523 votes to Landon's eight; the New Dealer also won the popular plurality of more than 11 million votes: 27,751,597 (60.8 percent) to Landon's 16,679,583.

An abundance of fringe parties fared poorly in 1936; the Union party under William Lemke disappointed with 882,479 votes and did a fast-fade from the national scene. The Socialists Norman Thomas managed only 187,750 and the Communist Party 80,150 for Earl Browder.

Samuel Elliot Morrison later wrote, "Before we dismiss Hoover from his unhappy four years in Washington to his happy thirty-one years of semi-retirement, we should remember that some degree of FDR's success in dealing with the depression, is owed to Hoover's proving that conventional methods had failed.

Collector's Choice
32nd President Franklin D. Roosevelt

"A Row of Democrats" 1940 trigate pictures ('R' for Roosevelt; 'O' for Sidney Osborn, Arizona candidate for Governor; 'W' for Henry Wallace, vice president, scarce coattail, b, w; 1¼ in.

"Don't Change the Pilot/Re-Elect F.D/ Roosevelt" FDR at ship's pilot wheel with Latin phrase "Fortis Non Timet," popular FDR labor litho; r, w; ⁷⁄₈ in.

"FDR You're Out at Third" one of the prime cartoon buttons; shows FDR as ball player being tagged out at third base as umpire signals "out"; b, w, blk.

"For Repeal and Prosperity" Roosevelt-Garner slogan jugate; r, w, b, blk; 1¼ in.

"Go 4th to Win the War" FDR picture button with stirring slogan; white reversed out of black; 1¼ in.

"Kick Out Depression with a Democratic Vote" choice mechanical button; cartoon donkey rears up to boot GOP elephant when string is pulled on donkey's nose; w, blk; 2¼ in.

"Let Freedom/Democracy Remain" FDR with conjoined sculptural bust of Washington and Jefferson; r, w, b; ⁷⁄₈ in.

"Roosevelt-Garner" jugate; stars and stripes border; r, w, b, blk: 1¼ in.

"FDR/Garner" bold white reversed out of blue cartoon of donkey; 1^1/4 in.

FDR–Garner, 1932; "For President Franklin D. Roosevelt & for Vice president John N. Garner" captioning seldom seen portraits; one of best post 1920's jugates; b, w; 1^1/4 in.

"FDR-Truman" 1944 jugate; stylized photos with stars; in black, dark brown; 1^1/4 in.

"Roosevelt," stunning oval name button of silhouetted FDR astride bucking bronco; "Not Teddy Roosevelt This Time." r, w; 2^3/4 in.

"For President/Franklin D. Roosevelt" choice wartime 1944 portrait pin with "V" (for Victory and Morse-code symbol flanking image/b, w; 2^1/4 in.

"Groundhogs of Virginia/Roosevelt" symbolism is unclear; may convey that pictured groundhog came out for FDR early—and proud of it; b, w; 2^1/8 in.

"He Is Worth a Buck to Me " caricature of grinning FDR smoking cigarette in holder; labor union contributor pin; Local 9, CIO Shipyard Workers issue; r, w, b, blk; 1^1/4 in.

FDR no-name pin; bust profile photo of FDR on telephone; b, w; 2 in.

"Railway Employees Roosevelt Club/Stark County, Ohio"; FDR picture on front of engine; r, blk, on pale gr; 1^1/4 in.

"Vote For Roosevelt," 1940 photo pin; r, b, w; 2^1/2 in.

Roosevelt no-name picture pin; image superimposed over vibrant red rose blossom; r, w, blk; ^{7}/8 in.

"Work and Wages/Roosevelt-Curley" jugate; tie-in with James Michael Curley, Mass. Item; multicolor; 1^3/4 in.

Alfred E. Landon,
GOP Nominee, 1936

"Landon-Knox" jugate; no sunflowers; b, w; 1^1/4 in.

"Young Republican Workers of New Jersey for Landon" scarce large Sunflower pin; b, br, y, w, gr; 2^1/2 in.

"Alf. M. Landon Notification/Topeka, July 23, 1936" photo pin with sunflower felt attached; blk, goldenrod; $2^3/8$ in.

Landon-Knox staggered portraits inside huge sunflower; mfgr. by Cruver; one of only four known; r, y, w, blk; 1 in.

"Landon Knox Out Roosevelt 1936"; Landon bluetone portrait; wordplay reversed out of blue border; b, w.

"Landon-Knox" Sunflower; one of the largest, most sought after of the Sunflower realm; b, y; $1^1/4$ in.

"Landon on the New Deal" GOP elephant squashing Democrat donkey cartoon pin; b, w, blk; $1^1/4$ in.

Landon Sunflower; Landon-Knox jugate, paper sunflower, with attached ribbons and tiny plastic elephant; large variant of common $^7/8$ in. button; goldenrod, br; $1^1/4$ in.

"Notification Day/Topeka, Kansas/Kansas City Will Win With Landon, July 3, 1936" "Compliments of Union League Club of Kansas City"; b, w, blk; 4 in.

Anti-Landon

"On the Rocks With Landon and Knox" slogan button; blk, w; $1^1/4$ in.

"We Can't Eat Sunflowers/Disgusted Republicans /Lets Lose With Landon" slogan bordered by sunflower petals; r, w, b, y: $2^1/8$ in.

39th Election—1940

President: Franklin D. Roosevelt (D)
Vice President: Henry Agard Wallace
Defeated candidates:
Wendell Willkie (R) and Charles McNary
Norman Thomas (S)
Roger Ward Babson (P)

Wendell Willkie launched his 1940 crusade against "the third term candidate, a president bent on perpetuating one-man rule." The third term specter failed to resonate with the populace, and it was only after Willkie pooh-poohed FDR's promise to stay out of the war that the Republican's "Keeping The Peace" movement really caught fire.

The GOP had nominated Wendell Willkie, a converted Democrat and utilities executive from Indiana, for the top slot; his running mate, Senate Minority Leader

Charles L. McNary of Oregon, was a friend of public power, though fairly conservative otherwise. FDR's choice for the second spot was controversial: Secretary of Agriculture Henry Wallace of Iowa, a militant New Dealer, and a promising vote-getter in the farm belt, had once been a Republican and some observers regarded him as a mystic.

FDR, in a ringing speech in Boston responded to charges of being a scheming war monger, "I have said this before, but I will say it again and again. Your boys are not going to be sent into foreign wars." FDR, like Wilson in 1914, could not keep his promise.

The turning point of the campaign, according to Willkie's Oren Root, founder of the Willkie Clubs, was FDR's ambassador to Great Britain, Joseph Kennedy's endorsement of FDR on CBS radio in late October, after originally promising his support for Willkie. (See "My Ambassador" button.)

Willkie was known as an able debater while in college and he challenged FDR to debate the issues. FDR insisted that he was too busy with other things and the country would wait another 20 years for presidential campaign debates.

In an unprecedented turnout of voters, FDR overwhelmed Willkie, carrying thirty-eight states, 449 electoral votes to Willkie's ten states, 82 electoral votes; FDR won 54.8 percent of the popular votes, 27,243,466 to 22,304,775. Norman Thomas of the Socialists won 99,557 and Roger Ward Babson, 57,812.

The 1940 race inspired a volume and variety of political trinketry promoting or insulting FDR and Willkie. It was without parallel in American annals with fifty-four million buttons issued by the two parties—thirty-three million by the GOP alone. Considering an influx of buttons peddled by commercial vendors, the GOP slogan buttons that claimed "100 Million Buttons Can't Be Wrong" may not be too great an exaggeration. To their sorrow, the GOP learned that campaign trinkets alone do not ordain victory.

Collector's Choice—Anti FDR

"De-thronement Day/November 5th"; y, b; $1^1/4$.

"Dr. Jekyll of Hyde Park"; b, w; $1^1/4$ in.

"8 Years Is Plenty"; white reversed out of black billiard 8-ball; b, w; 1¹/4 in.

"My Ambassador"; refers to FDR's Ambassador to England, Joseph Kennedy, who made the private boast he would put "25 million Catholic votes behind Willkie to throw FDR out." b, w; 1¹/4 in.

"My Day/(the Name of Eleanor's syndicated column), When I Vote for Willkie"; b, w; 1¹/4 in.

"My Friend/I'm Indispensable" w, b; 1¹/4 in.

"Napoleon Met His Waterloo/Frank You Will Too"; pale blue, blk; 1¹/4 in.

"No Man Is Good a Third time"; b,w; 1 /4 in.

"No International Third Reich Third Term" r, w; 1¹/4 in.

"No Third Term" cartoon of Uncle Sam turning thumbs down; r, w, b; ⁷/8 in.

"I'm Against the 3rd Term/Washington Wouldn't/Grant Couldn't/Roosevelt Shouldn't"; r, w, b; 1¹/4 in.

"Roosevelt/Hide At Hyde" reference to FDR residence at Hyde Park, New York; o, blk; 1¹/4.

"Roosevelt Would Rather Be President Than Right"; a reverse twist on Henry Clay's famous statement; o, blk; 1¹/4 in.

"Rotten Eggs with Roosevelt/Omelettes With Willkie"; b, w; 1¹/4 in.

"Worst Public Administration" slogan emphasizes first letters of each word to spell out the "WPA" an FDR pet project; w,b; 1¹/4 in.

Collector's Choice
Wendell Willkie, GOP Nominee, 1940

There are four known Willkie and McNary jugates, although a fifth version, a variant in which Willkie's name is misspelled "Willke" has also turned up; the only example known.

"I'm for Willkie and McNary" jugate bust portraits; b, w; ⁷/8 in.

"The American Way of life" Willkie-McNary jugate; with large US flag above: r, w, b; 1 in.

"Wendell Willkie for President; Charles McNary For Vice-president"; jugate; r, w, b; $^7/_8$ in.

"Confucius Say Willkie OK" slogan button; b, w; 1$^1/_4$ in.

"Each Time He Needs Him/God Sends a Man/Wendell Willkie" bust portrait; messianic message appeared on GOP National Convention pin; r, w, blk; $^7/_8$ in.

"East Side/West Side/Wants Willkie" slogan inside large brown derby; alluding to Democrat Al Smith's endorsement of Willkie; brown, w; 1$^1/_4$ in.

"God Bless America" Willkie photo button; seldom used reference to the deity; b, w; 1$^1/_4$ in.

"*Guard Our Peace*" slogan runs in three rows with first letters spelling GOP; b, w; 1$^1/_4$ in.

"Life begins in '40/Willkie/GOP Women/Shawnee County" GOP elephant cartoon; r, w, b; $^7/_8$ in.

"The Hope of Our Country/Wendell Willkie" Wilkie portrait with draped flag framing button; r, w, b; 1$^1/_4$ in.

"Willkie Square Deal" slogan inside blue and red square; b, r; $^7/_8$ in.

"Willkie and Chemurgy" stylized view of plants, farm, houses and forms of transportation; multicolor (one of the modern classics); 1$^1/_4$ in.

"Willkie" 1940 cartoon pin picturing Red Schoolhouse; r, w, b; $^7/_8$ in.

Willkie-ite"single picture button with Capitol in b g; r, w, b; $^7/_8$ in.

40th Election—1944

President: Franklin D. Roosevelt
Vice President: Harry S. Truman
Defeated candidates:
Thomas E. Dewey (R) and John Bricker
Norman Thomas (S)
Claude A. Watson (P)

The 1944 election was the first wartime presidential contest since the Lincoln-McClellan Civil War tilt eighty years earlier. FDR appeared steadfast in wishing to remain at the helm. Party opposition to 1940 running mate Henry Wallace so intensified that FDR would settle for "the new Missouri Compromise," Harry S Truman. Wallace's vice-presidential replacement was a protégé of machine boss Tom Pentergast who won a Senate seat in 1934 and gained national attention as chairman of a special committee to investigate defense spending.

In the Chicago GOP convention, after an early surge for war hero General Douglas MacArthur, the nomination went to Thomas E. Dewey, governor of New York and a former District Attorney with a reputation as relentless racket buster. Also chosen on the first ballot as a vice-presidential candidate was John W. Bricker, Conservative governor of Ohio.

Although FDR appeared apathetic at the campaign's off-set, he suddenly came alive late in September. Rankled by the frequent assaults on his record, he delivered a speech to the Teamsters in Washington D.C. on September 23, that many regard as the finest campaign rhetoric of his career. FDR regaled the GOP "who suddenly discover every four years, just before election day, that they love labor, after having attacked it for three years and six months."

Though pollsters predicted a close election, FDR breezed in again, carrying thirty-six states with 432 votes in the Electoral College to Dewey's 99; in a popular vote walkover, the war-year president topped Dewey 25,602,504 to 22,006,285. Afterward, FDR quipped, "the first twelve years are the hardest."

On January 20, 1945, FDR took his oath of office for the fourth time. Less than a year later, he died of a cerebral hemorrhage on April 12, and Harry Truman assumed the reins.

With metals and plastics in critical short supply on the home front during wartime, the 1944 contest proved a singularly bleak one for campaign items. Only a hundred or so varieties of pinbacks and other lapel devices appeared with an influx of mini-banners and paper stickers or decals.

The fourth-term issue inspired surprisingly few buttons. FDR meanwhile milked patriotism frenzy to a "fare thee well," many of them flashing the famous "V" symbol for Victory and the alliterative "Go 4th to Win The War."

Collector's Choice—Franklin D. Roosevelt, 1944

"Roosevelt–Truman" large patriotic shield with heads representing members of various Armed forces; r, w, b, gold; $1^1/4$ in.

41st Election—1948

President: Harry S. Truman
Vice President: Alban Barkley
Defeated candidates:
Thomas E. Dewey and John Bricker
J. Strom Thurmond (STR) and Fielding Wright

Political pundits dismissed incumbent Harry Truman with the one-liner, "To err is Truman," but the interim president who filled in following FDR's fatal stroke fooled naysayers by reviving an old FDR coalition of farmers, workers, ethnics and the South.

Fifty of the nation's leading political writers picked Dewey as the winner. The pollsters had the GOP nominee ahead by a wide margin. Odds-makers declared Dewey a 15 to 1 shoo-in.

The outlook appeared even bleaker, when after the Democrats had enthusiastically endorsed Truman on the convention floor, for his courageous stand on civil rights, thirty-five delegates (all of Mississippi's and half of Alabama's) stalked out of the convention. They (the "Dixiecrats") later nominated South Carolina Governor J. Strom Thurmond and Mississippi Governor Fielding Wright for their slate.

Unfazed and utterly convinced he could win voters to his cause, Truman embarked on a strenuous campaign, barnstorming the country and logging 21,928 miles and delivering nearly 300 speeches.

The total vote turnout was down as only 50.2 percent went to the polls in 1948. On November 2, Truman received a plurality of over 2 million popular votes (24,105,812 to 21,970,065) carried 28 states—303 electoral votes to Dewey 16 —-189 votes. Strom Thurmond's States Rights Party accounted for 38 electoral votes and 1,169,021 in the popular. Henry Wallace's Progressive/American Laborites finished with 1,156,103.

On Oct. 5, 1947 Harry Truman became the first president to deliver a live telecast; he also was the first to have horseshoe pitching tents constructed on White House grounds.

Collector's Choice—33rd President
Harry S Truman

Short on funds and with all but a few faithful not wanting to be linked with an almost certain loser, Truman campaign items were greatly outnumbered by those from the Dewey camp.

The Democrats dominant theme–the continuation of economic achievements and liberal initiatives of the New Deal—was perhaps best expressed in a colorful poster picturing Herbert Hoover, which warned "Don't Monkey With the Donkey in '48 or Sell Hoover Apples in '49."

Anti-Truman

"Behind The 8-Ball" 1948; blacktone image of HST superimposed pool ball; b, w; $1^1/_2$ in.

"Truman was Screwy to Build a Front Porch for Dewey" slogan pin; b, cr; $1^1/_4$ in.

"Don't Tarry/Vote Harry" slogan button 1948; b, w; $1^1/_4$ in.

"Forward with Truman/No Retreat" 1948 slogan button; (scarce item made by Geo. J. Reid Co, Milwaukee); b, w; 2 in.

"I'm Just Wild About 'Harry'"1948, Democrats used famous song in slogan button, centered by large star; b, w; $3^1/_2$ in.

"Give 'Em H———, Harry" Souvenir pin of Gov. Orville L. Freeman Appreciation Dinner, Dec. 10, 1955; b, w; 2 in.

"60 Million People Working/Why Change?" 1948 Truman picture button; b, w; 2 in.

"Truman-Barkley" red donkey cartoon, r, w; $1^1/_2$ in.

"Truman Crusader" acrostic letters inside Cross; 1948 key item; r, w, b; $1^1/_4$ in.

"Very Truly Yours/Harry S. Truman" in script below portrait of young HST 1930s; Truman for Missouri district court judge-scarcest of all HST; sepia; 4 in.

"Westminster College/Harry Truman/Winston Churchill, Fulton, Mo. 1946" one of several word pin variants, commemorates historic meeting between two world leaders; Churchill coined phrase, Iron Curtain/r, w, b; 2 in.

Collector's Choice—Thomas E. Dewey, GOP Nominee in 1944 and 1948

"Dewey the Racket Buster/New Deal Buster" 1944 slogan pin; w, blk; 1¹/4 in.

"Dewey-Bricker" 1948; jugate; r, w, b; 1 in.

"Dewey–Warren" 1944; jugate; w, blk; 1¹/4 in.

"God Bless America/Dewey/ 1944" Dewey portrait r, gray, b; 1¹/4 in.

Thomas Dewey Portrait Pin, 1948; black, white; 1¹/4 in.

Buttons that attempted to gain some mileage on HST's recent civil rights initiatives espoused "Truman and Civil Rights," "Truman Fights For Human Rights," and "States Rights or Human Rights?" (A swipe at the Dixiecrats).

Truman's prickly relationship with the GOP-dominated 80th Congress (he called them the "Do-Nothing" Congress) is reflected in a button stating "The Won't Do Congress Won't Do."

1948 was a banner year for third party items and for trinkets trumpeting major party hopefuls' buttons were issued for Democrats Richard Russell and Paul McNutt and reluctant draftees Justice William O. Douglas and Gen. Dwight Eisenhower. Pinbacks surfaced for perennial contender Harold Stassen and Earl Warren, i.e, "Bases Loaded/Warren Is Scorin.'" Among thirty items inspired by the General Douglas MacArthur boomlet, pinbacks anointed him "America's Hero" and "The Man of the Hour" and "Save America with McArthur." Segregationist Dixiecrats Strom Thurmond and Fielding Wright running on the States Rights ticket promoted "For a Free People Under Constitutional Government" tabs and "Jeffersonian Democrat" buttons.

Henry Wallace, FDR's cast-off vice president from 1940, running in '48 as a Progressive, is known for at least thirty varieties of buttons, including one extolling "Wallace/One World" and "Repeal Taft-Hartley."

Other Henry Wallace entries:

"Seamen for Wallace"; stylized merchant marine ship";
w, b, blk: 1¹/4 in.

42ⁿᵈ Election—1952

President: Dwight D. Eisenhower (R)
Vice President: Richard M. Nixon
Defeated candidates:
Adlai Ewing Stevenson (D) and John Sparkman
Vincent Halliman (PR)
Stuart Hamblen (PR)

The Democratic nominee for 1952, Adlai Stevenson II,
governor of Illinois, was a grandson of Adlai Stevenson,
a vice president, under Cleveland in 1893. The glib-
tongued governor talked himself into the leading candidate's role to test a seemingly unbeatable World War II
war hero candidate, the enormously popular Dwight
D."Ike" Eisenhower of Texas, a moderate, critical of the
welfare state but willing to accept New Deal reforms.

The GOP felt they had a foolproof formula for victory: the
Korean War, corruption, and Communism as they crucial
issues.

The General's major bombshell came late in the campaign when he announced he would end the war in Korea
if he became president. Though the Democrats dismissed it as a grandstand gesture, "for all intents and
purposes," wrote one journalist, "the contest ended that
night."

The Democrats balanced the ticket with John Sparkman,
a New Deal senator from Alabama as nominee.

Ike's running mate, Richard Nixon, a California senator,
had just weathered a major crisis when the *New York
Post* revealed that a group of wealthy Californians had set
up a sizeable "slush fund" of over $18,000 when Nixon
served in the Senate. Nixon took his appeal to the nation
on prime time TV with his impassioned "Checkers"
speech in which he disavowed any wrongdoing, adding
that "regardless of what they say about it, the Nixons
were going to keep our gift of a little black and white
spotted cocker spaniel named Checkers." The convincing speech attracted the largest TV audience up to that
time.

Along with extremists such as senators William Jenner of Indiana and Joe McCarthy of Wisconsin, Nixon could be counted on to do the down-and-dirty campaigning, while Ike perfected his fatherly image.

Eisenhower won a victory of epic proportions, again stunning the pollsters as to the extent of his plurality—more than 6.5 million votes. Ike won 55.4 per cent of the popular votes, 33,824,351 to 27,314,987 and carried 30 states with 442 electoral votes and significantly, became the first Republican since Hoover to make inroads in the Deep South by winning five states. Vincent Halliman of the Progressive/American Labor finished a distant third at 132,608.

43rd Election—1956

President: Dwight Eisenhower(R)
Vice President: Richard Nixon
Defeated candidates:
Adlai Stevenson and Estes Kefauver
Coleman Andrews (ISR)
Harry F. Byrd (I)

Adlai Stevenson launched the less than sparkling 1956 race with a scathing criticism of Eisenhower's foreign policy, pointing to the GOP's "liberation policy" that recklessly encouraged uprisings in the Middle East and Eastern Europe, but when they revolted, the United States could do nothing to help the insurgents without risking war with Russia. These attacks evoked little change in voter attitudes.

The Middle East crisis may actually have even strengthened Eisenhower's position with the American people. In time of crisis, many observers argued, it was dangerous to change presidents and Ike, with his vast military expertise, was the right man in the right place.

Eisenhower had suffered a heart attack in September 1955, but made an excellent recovery, and announced he would seek a second term. The GOP meeting in San Francisco renominated Ike by acclamation and picked Nixon again for vice president.

Stevenson was challenged for the top spot at the Democratic Convention in Chicago by Senator Estes Kefauver of Tennessee. On the strength of a decisive victory in California, Stevenson secured the nomination on the first ballot. In an eloquent acceptance speech, Stevenson called for "A New America" where "poverty is abolished."

Kefauver settled for the second slot, although John F. Kennedy, a junior Senator from Massachusetts, made an impressive showing in the early balloting.

The margin of victory was even more lopsided than in the 1952 race. The GOP electoral cushion was 457 to 74; Ike's 35,582,236 popular votes dwarfed Stevenson's 26,028,887. Independent States' Righter T. Coleman Andrews won 275,915 votes.

The election was hailed as a triumph of Modern Republicanism but in reality, it was another personal triumph for the 66-year-old president. Ike outran the Republican Congressional ticket by over 6.5 million votes and the Democrats took control of both the House and Senate.

The 34th U.S. President, Dwight Eisenhower, was one of the ablest and most personable men ever elected president and the people endorsed his first term by reelecting him with even greater majorities in 1956. Everyone, as an outpouring of campaign buttons confirmed, "Liked Ike." But consciously or unconsciously, he emerged as a constitutional monarch, a symbolic chief of state as opposed to a dynamic initiator of policy.

Collector's Choice—34th President Dwight D. Eisenhower

"Ike/One Good Term Deserves Another" slogan pin; r, w, b; 1³/₄ in.

"I Like Ike/But Who Likes Bill" 1952 pre-convention pin; slant is that Ike preferred Nixon over Bill Knowland for No. 2 slot; b, goldenrod; 4 in.

"Eisenhower/Nixon" reverse out of red bust jugate; r, w, b, blk; 1¹/₄.

"Ike/Dick/Don't change the team in the middle of the stream" head photos of Ike and Dick. Revival of an 1864 Republican slogan; r, b, blk; 3¹/₂ in.

"Ike/Dick/Sure to Click" jugate; r, w, b, blk; 2¹/₂ in.

"Ike and Dick Women's Nat'l Republican Club" '52 jugate photos; r, cr, b, blk; 3¹/₂ in.

"My Friend Ike" Civil Rights pin shows black and white hands clasping under photo of Ike; blk, br, w; 1¼ in.

"Re-elect Eisenhower/Nixon/ Peace, Progress, Prosperity" jugate (slogan used in the 1920 Cox race)1956; r, w, b, blk; 3½ in.

"Riders Of '52 For Ike" identity of "riders," is a mystery; a colorful, elusive slogan button; Ike pedaled to a big win; y, scarlet; 2¼ in.

"Time For a Change" 1952 no-name cartoon variant of pin pictured above has baby facing viewer; r, y, blk; 4 in.

Standout among deluge of '52 "I Like Ike" entries; black, white 1¼ in. (42nd election.)

1956 Eisenhower/Nixon

"Will Spike for Ike" Monongahela Railroad employees support Ike; slogan pin; r, w, b, swirl design, 1¾ in.

"New Jersey for Eisenhower" slogan over white silhouette of state; r, blk, gld; 1¼ in. Examples are known for all 48 states; New Jersey rates as the scarcest.

"I Like 'Ike'" five star General; with star cluster above lettering; perhaps the best embodying this famous slogan; r, w, b; 1¼ in.

Ike Sign Language pin; most coveted of all Ike language pins; uses hand signals; r, w, b; ¼ in.

"You Like Ike/We Love Him"; b, w; 3½ in.

Collector's Choice—Adlai E. Stevenson, Democratic Nominee for 1952 and 1956

"Adlai And Estes—The Bestest/The Winning Team," catchy slogan button with images of Stevenson and vice-president mate Kefauver in four leaf clover with virtues, i.e., "Maturity, Integrity" in each leaf; boasts that AES is strongest in South, and EK is strongest in Farm Belt; g, w, blk; 3 in.

"A Winning Team/Stevenson/Kefauver" jugate b, w, 2¾ in. oval.

"Dollars For Democrats"; Stevenson-Kefauver TV jugate; w, blk; 2 in.

"For '56," crossed leg cartoon rebus with one shoe to show Stevenson's famous hole in sole; w, blk,

"I Like Stevenson," Bill Mauldin's famed Joe of *Willie & Joe Up-Front* cartoon; r, w, blk; 1^1/$_4$ in.

"I'm for Stevenson/How We'd Like to See Harry"; portrait of Truman with lip buttoned; humorous way of discouraging HST from antagonizing voters while stumping for Stevenson; r, w, blk; 2^1/$_2$ in.

"I'm Still Madly For Adlai"; 1956 bust of Stevenson; b, w; 2^1/$_8$ in.

"My Favorite Sun (sun rebus) is Stevenson"; w, o, blk; 1^1/$_2$ in.

"The Team for You/Not Just the Few" trigate of "Adlai" (Stevenson, "Estes" (Kefaufer) and "George"(Rhodes) Pennsylvania Congressman candidate; 1956 coattail; r, w, b; 4 in.

"We Cannot Afford a Lesser Man/Stevenson for President" 1960 single picture draft Sevenson pin; w. blue-tone; 1^1/$_4$ in.

"We've Still Got Steve Up Our Sleeves," cartoon of laughing donkey in circle; y, blk; 2^1/$_4$ in.

"Why Be Fooled By the Old Bunk in a New Trunk/Vote Democratic," elephant with raised trunk squirting water; r, w, b; 3^1/$_4$ in.

44th Election—1960

President: John F. Kennedy (D)
Vice President: Lyndon Baines Johnson
Defeated candidates:
Richard M. Nixon
Henry Cabot Lodge

John F. Kennedy, a senator from Massachusetts and a Roman Catholic, had narrowly missed out as Stevenson's running mate in 1956 before Estes Kefauver prevailed in the third ballot in an open convention.

Senator Hubert Humphrey of Minnesota provided the major opposition in the 1960s primaries, but withdrew after JFK won decisively in seven widely scattered states and in both the Wisconsin and West Virginia primaries proving he could do well among Protestant voters.

Kennedy's closest rival for the presidential nod at the Democratic convention, Texas Senator Lyndon Johnson, was offered and accepted the second slot.

Richard Nixon, who had remained in Ike's shadow for eight years, was nominated on the first ballot with Henry Cabot Lodge, chief US representative to the United Nations for second place.

Pivotal in 1960 was the first televised series of debates between major presidential contestants. JFK, who lacked the national exposure of Nixon, appeared to undergo an amazing transformation, starting out as a "wet behind the ears" underdog and winding up upstaging Nixon, by coming off more self-assured and quick and concise under verbal fire.

TV cameras were unkind to Nixon, who gave the appearance of having a heavy black beard, dark eyes, hanging jowls and ski-jump nose, in sharp contrast to poster boy JFK.

A major disappointment for Nixon was his failure to receive a full-fledged endorsement from his ex-boss. When asked in a press conference, what major decisions his vice president had participated in, Eisenhower exclaimed, "If you give me a week, I might think of one." Only in the waning days of the race did Ike belatedly step in to lend his immense prestige to the Nixon cause.

Late in the race, civil rights leader Martin Luther King, Jr. was arrested with fifty-two other blacks for trying to desegregate a restaurant in Atlanta. When JFK heard the news he at once telephoned Mrs. King and his brother Robert got in touch with the judge to secure King's release on bail. Nixon, after discussing the case with Eisenhower's attorney-general, declined to intervene. JFK's action triggered a warm response and undoubtedly, this mobilized the black vote in his favor.

In the largest voter turnout in the nation's history, JFK emerged the winner at 43, the youngest man to be elected president. The final count: 303 electoral votes to Nixon's 219 and the closest popular vote since the 1888 Cleveland-Harrison race: 34,227,096 to Nixon's 34,107,646.

The Independent Party's Harry Byrd picked up 15 electoral votes and States Rightist Orval Faubus won 214,549 in the popular tally.

Collector's Choice—35th President
John F. Kennedy

A number of varieties of sterling silver figural PT-109 patrol boat lapel pins were passed out sparingly to friends and dignitaries and campaign workers commemorating JFK's heroism in the South Pacific during World War II, and rank among the most popular 1960 campaign items.

"*A Profile In Courage*/Elect US Senator John F. Kennedy"; one of few references to JFK's Pulitzer Prize winning book; from 1956, when he was on the A-list as possible vice-president nominee; b, w; 2¹/4 in.

"All the Way with JFK/Kennedy for President" 1960; r, w, b, blk, 1¹/4 in.

"America Needs Kennedy" portrait flasher JFK in other view; w, blk; 2¹/4 in.

Atomic Years Button; JFK profile silhouette; b, w; 2¹/4 in.

"Elect Kennedy President" youthful 1960 button; b, w; 2¹/8 in.

"Just for Kinfolk" slogan spelled out from vertical use of JFK in large letters; Nation's Capitol in b g; r, w, b, blk: 3³/4 in.

"Keep Up With the Kennedy's" slogan inside shamrock; g, w; 1¹/2 in.

"Lets Back Jack" cartoon head of JFK; b, w, blk; 2³/4 in.

"Kennedy for President" Kennedy portrait flasher; multicolor; 2 in.

"Kennedy Johnson/America's Men For The '60s"; r, w, blk; 6 in.

"Kennedy/He Will Win" flasher portrait button of JFK; w, blk; 1³/4 in.

"JFK-Jackie Kennedy" no name matching portrait button in wreath like frame; w, blk; 1¹/4 in.

"Leadership for the 60s/Kennedy-Johnson"; r, w, b; rectangular litho; 2¹/8 x 3 in.

"Our Next President" portrait of JFK supered against U.S. flag; r, w, b, blk; 4 in.

"Progress for All/Forward With Kennedy"; JFK bust portrait supered over large shield; r, w, b, blk; 1³/4 in.

"Shoeworkers for Kennedy" portrait button of smiling JFK; r, w, b, blk; 3¹/2 in.

"Start Packing Mamie/The Kennedy's Are Coming" slogan button; r, b, blk; 3¹/2 in.

"Viva Kennedy" large Mexican sombrero with slogan across crown; r, y, blk: 1¹/4 in.

"Vote Straight Democratic Ticket"; Kennedy-Johnson jugate; r, w, b, blk; 3 in.

"Youth for Kennedy" photo button; Senate race issue; r, w, blk; 2¹/4 in.

Anti-JFK

"Members *Sons Of Business Society*" cartoon of mournful looking basset hound; prompted by offhand JFK remark that businessmen were S.O.B's. (any number of

John F. Kennedy's Pulitzer Prize-winning book is evoked in 1956 white, black; 1/4 in. button.

1960 John F. Kennedy, the Atomic Years, red, white, blue, 1 3/4 in. classic (43rd Election).

1960 John Kennedy PT 109 silver stud.

slogan buttons bearing the initials were issued); 1962; w, blk; 1³/4 in.

"Prostitutes for Nixon and Kennedy" slogan in script; vendor salesman's safety pin; w, blk; 2 in.

"What Would You Like to be Son?/President Dad,/I Mean When You Grow Up?" cartoon of toothy JFK in small boy's sailor suit and hat; w, blk: 4¹/2 in.

45ᵗʰ Election—1964

President: Lyndon B. Johnson (D)
Vice President: Hubert Humphrey
Defeated candidates:
Barry Goldwater (R) and William Miller
Eric Hass (SL)
Clifton DeBerry (SW)

With John F. Kennedy's assassination on November 22, 1963, Lyndon Johnson assumed the mantle and the New Frontier evanesced into the Great Society. The Democrats lost little time in securing passage of the historic Civil Rights Act of 1964 and other legislation critical to LBJ's "War On Poverty."

The GOP offered voters "A choice not an echo," in ultra conservative Barry M. Goldwater, a Senator from Arizona and the first Jewish major party candidate for high office. "In Your Heart, You Know He's Right" chanted the Goldwaterites, a slogan reiterated on thousands of campaign buttons. (Democrats countered with a button that got a lot of guffaws, "In Your Guts You Know He's Nuts.")

The Republicans' choice for vice president was a little known Congressman from upstate New York, William Miller, a Roman Catholic. The Democrats chose Hubert Humphrey, a senior Senator from Minnesota.

The 1964 campaign saw the Democrats constantly putting Goldwater on the defensive as "he shot from the lip." Goldwater was never able to fully explain a phrase that came back to haunt him throughout the campaign: "Extremism in defense of liberty is no vice."

At the end of September, LBJ who'd maintained a low profile, could no longer restrain himself, taking to the stump and crisscrossing the country for forty-two days, covering over 60,000 miles, pressing the flesh and delivering almost two hundred speeches promising peace and prosperity.

Lyndon Johnson and Barry Goldwater forces took turns accusing the other of being "trigger happy" in Vietnam in 1964; black, white; $7/8$ in.

Johnson repeatedly assured voters he did not intend to get involved in Vietnam, but following a brief encounter between US warships and North Vietnam patrol craft in the Gulf of Tonkin, he persuaded Congress to pass a resolution authorizing him to "take all necessary steps" including the use of armed force to assist South Vietnam and "prevent aggression."

The sound state of the economy helped LBJ with the rich; his war on poverty helped him with the poor. Sighed one GOP leader, "I can't remember a time when a President had prosperity and poverty going for him at the same time."

LBJ achieved his heart's desire—a gullywasher win—the most decisive since FDR overwhelmed Landon in 1936. Johnson carried forty-four states and the District of Columbia, (voting for the first time in accord with the 23rd Amendment) 486 to 52 in the Electoral College; popular plurality was over 16 million, 43,126,218 to Goldwater's 27,174,898. Eric Hass of the Socialist-Labor party: 32,720 won 45,219 and the Socialist Workers' Clinton DeBerry.

Collector's Choice
36th President Lyndon B. Johnson
"Let Us Continue" conjoining images of JFK and Lyndon Johnson; a poignant reminder of the changing of the guard after Kennedy's assassination; r, w, and pale blue; 3 in. classic.

"Let Us Continue/Vote Democratic" LBJ and JFK portraits inside white star with image of mortar and pestle; r, w, b; 3 in.

"Me and Roosevelt for Johnson" 1937 Texas coattail jugate paired with FDR; LBJ won run-off for Congressional

seat following death of incumbent James Buchanan; r, w, b, 2¹/4 in.

"Young Citizens for Johnson" cartoon of Democrats; donkey with r, w, b, zebra stripes; 2¹/4 in. classic

Collector's Choice—Anti-Johnson

Button producers laid-off Richard Nixon, but acid-tongued LBJ versions included:

"Supersam/Get Out of Viet Nam" stylized LBJ as Superman.

"Write-in Lyndon Baines Johnson for Coroner" slogan button.

"King Lyndon the First" unflattering caricature of LBJ wearing crown; r, w, blk; 1¹/4 in.

"Strangelove Lives" LBJ in dark glasses reprises Peter Sellers role; b, w; 7/8 in.

"All the Way with LBJ/But Don't Go Near the YMCA" tasteless anti-Johnson button refers to LBJ's aide Walter Jenkins' homosexual incident; w, blk; 1¹/2 in.

"A Page from My Past/My Strong Right Arm" cartoon of LBJ aide Bobby Baker who was investigated by Senate for shady dealings; b,w, blk; 3 in.

Barry Goldwater, Republican Nominee 1964 Collector's Choice

"Extremism In the Defense of Liberty Is No Vice; Moderation in the Pursuit of Justice Is No Virtue/Goldwater in '64"; single Goldwater picture button with a dictum that came back to haunt him; black w, with red rim; 1¹/4 in.

"Goldwater in '64"; picture of Air Force fighter plane flown by Reservist pilot Goldwater; gld, w, blk; 1¹/4 in.

"I Am a Right Wing Extremist" slogan pin; w, blk; 7/8 in.

"I'm a Beattles Fan. In Case of Emergency Place My Vote For Barry" slogan button; w, blk; 3¹/2 in.

"It Needs Goldwater for Good Roots" line drawing of "The Democratic Lyndon Tree" with roots labeled "Bobby

Baker, Racial Violence, Cuba; Foreign Failures, Billy Estes; High Gov't Spending, Forgotten Constitution"; gld, blk; $1^1/4$ in.

"The Goldwater Band Wagon Is rolling Along/Hop On!" slogan button; black on white; 2 in.

"Save America/Vote Republican/Goldwater/Miller" jugate with furled r, w, b banners; r, w, b, blk; $1^1/4$ in.

Collector's Choice—Anti-Goldwater

"Dr. Strangewater For President" cartoon button; $1^1/4$ in.

"Goldwater for Halloween" slogan button; black on orange; $1^1/4$ in.

"In Your Guts You Know He's Nuts" slogan button; w, blk; $1^1/4$ in.

"Goldwater-Miller" jugate; b, w with r, w, b, rim; $1^3/4$ in.

"A Great Day for the USA With Goldwater For President"; single picture button; b, w, blk; 2 in.

"Au H20'64" illustration of larger glass of water with chemical symbol oveprinted; w, y, blk; 2 in.

"Barry" cartoon of dinosaur wearing Goldwater's trademarked glasses; w, blk; $2^1/8$ in.

"What—Me Worry?" bluetone of Goldwater superimposed over mushroom cloud; blk, w; $2^1/8$ in.

46th Election—1968

President: Richard M. Nixon (R)
Vice President: Spiro T. Agnew
Defeated candidates:
Hubert Humphrey (D) and Edmund Muskie
George Wallace (A) and Gen. Curtiss LeMay

Richard Nixon, now 55, staged a remarkable comeback in 1968. Considered a lame duck following his devastating loss to John Kennedy in 1960 and his failure to win the governorship of California in 1962, Nixon again found his place in the sun at the GOP Convention in Miami Beach. He handily staved off challenges from Governors Ronald Reagan of California and Nelson Rockefeller of New York to win the top spot on the first ballot. "Spiro Who?" Agnew, governor of Maryland, was nominated as vice president.

The Democrats in Chicago, nominated LBJ's vice-president, Hubert Humphrey, a golden-tongued orator who earned the nickname "Minnesota Chats." The frontrunner, Humphrey's acceptance speech, "the politics of happiness and joy" came off as singularly uninspiring, in light of a fractious convention clearly divided between hawks and doves.

Senator Edmund Muskie of Maine accepted the runner-up slot. The bloody police skirmish with anti-Vietnam demonstrators at Chicago's Democratic Convention badly hurt Humphrey's cause.

1968—Tragic and troubled times

A number of tumultuous incidents leading up to the November election had a profound influence on its outcome. On March 31, LBJ stunned the nation when he announced, "I will not seek and will not accept the nomination of my party for another term." On April 27, Civil Rights Leader Martin Luther King, Jr. was felled by an assassin in Memphis and his death touched off an orgy of rioting that would have appalled the beloved apostle of non-violence. Then on June 6, Sen. Robert F. Kennedy of New York was murdered in Los Angeles by a young Arab nationalist, just as his chances for the Democratic nomination had skyrocketed with a win in the California primary.

Nixon's stance on integration and law and order was so strikingly akin to the views of American Independence Party candidate Governor George Wallace of Alabama, they both found themselves appealing to the same voters in the Deep South.

Humphrey tried desperately to remove himself from LBJ's Vietnam policy. It wasn't until late September, however, that Humphrey finally took a stronger stand, calling for a cessation in bombing and de-escalation of the war. In doing so, he received the support of fellow Democrats Edward Kennedy, Eugene McCarthy, George McGovern and other doves. Humphrey finally became fired up, tearing into the Wallace-General LeMay as the "bombsey twins" and called Nixon "Richard the Chickenhearted" for refusing to debate him.

Humphrey's last minute bombast may have given his chances a temporary bump, but it was too little, too late. More than 73 million went to the polls and chose Richard Nixon, who carried 32 states with 302 electoral votes to

Humphrey's 14 with 191 votes; the popular vote was tighter, with Nixon edging HHH by only 510,315 or 31,275,165 (43.3 percent) to 31,266,996 (42.7 percent.) Wallace fared exceptionally well as an American Independent, gaining 9,899,567 with 46 electoral votes, the best showing ever by a splinter-party. In 1971 the 26th Amendment was enacted, lowering the voting age to 18 in all elections.

Collector's Choice—37th President
Richard M. Nixon

"Even the Great Pumpkin Is Voting Nixon–Agnew" door hanger; o, b, blk;

"It's Time to Elect Nixon President" slogan pin with "Nixon" repeated four times to form a square clock face and dial pointing to five minutes to twelve; (one of the classic Nixons); r, w, b; 2^1/$_8$ in.

"Man Of Steel" Nixon bust profile showpiece; 1960; r, blk, w; 3^1/$_2$ in.

"Nixon in November" strong graphic with giant letter "N" photo button, 1960; r, w, b; 6 in.

"Nixon in '68/Give America Another Great President"; Nixon portrait with cameo images of Washington, Lincoln and Teddy Roosevelt; r, wh, b, blk; 2^1/$_4$ in.

Nixon/Lodge/Vote Republican, 1960 jugate; r, w, blk, gld.

"Nixon's the One," witty cartoon spoof on a favorite Nixon motto; leading race with also-rans, Hubert Humphrey and George Wallace; r, b, blk; 1^1/$_4$ in.

"Re-elect the President" 1964; Nixon with wide grin bust photo; r, b, blk; 3 in.

1968 Richard Nixon has lead on Hubert Humphrey and George Wallace in 1968 race; red, white, light blue, black; 1¾ in. (46th Election).

Humphrey googly-eyes; blk, g, w; 3½ in.

"Join the Nixon New Revolution"; r, w, b; 3 in.

"Keep Dick on the Job" 1964 Nixon portrait; r, w, b, blk; 3½ in.

"He's Good Enough for Me" "In '68/Nixon" finger-pointing Uncle Sam cartoon figure with smiling Nixon, recalls Teddy Roosevelt 1904 version; r, w, b, blk; 2¼ in.

"Nixon in '68/Give America Another Great President" bust of Nixon with images of Lincoln, Washington, and T. Roosevelt; r, w, b, blk; 1¼ in.

Collector's Choice—Anti-Nixon
Gone With the Wind tasteless anti-Nixon cartoon of Democrat's Donkey passing gas, encircling image of Nixon; blk, y; 3 in.

"I Have Nothing to Hide!" Nixon streaking in buff, flashing V-sign cartoon; Watergate item; r, b; 1¼ in.

"Is Agnew a Sure Bet?" slogan button B-spelling out-Bribery; E-Extortion and T-Tax Evasion"; b, w; 2 in. (Agnew's resignation in '73 gave button vendors a field day.)

Collector's Choice—Hubert H. Humphrey, Democratic Nominee, 1968
"Capitol City/St. Paulitans for Humphrey" 1968 shows HHH superimposed over skyscraper Minnesota state capitol building; gld, b, blk; 1½ in.

"'HHH' Fills the prescription" cartoon of Humphrey exploiting his former profession as pharmacist with medicine vials; b, w, blk; 1¼ in.

"R/X Vote for a Better World/Humphrey & Muskie '68/Democratic" slogan button; blk, b; 1¼ in.

"Save America/Vote Democrat" Humphrey-Muskie jugate; r, w, b, blk; $1^1/_4$ in.

Collector's Choice—Anti-Humphrey

"Don't Get Humphed in '68/ Vote Republican"; vendor button, w, blk; $1^1/_4$ in.

"Dump the Hump" psychedelic slogan; r, w; $^7/_8$ in.

"This is No Yoke" Humphrey cartoon sitting on wall as in Humpty Dumpty nursery rhyme; b, w; $1^1/_2$ in.

Other anti's read: "Chicken Little Laid Hubert H. Humphrey"; "Why Trade the Ventriloquist for the Dummy!"; "Hawk/Hypocrite/H-Bomber"

1948 Henry A. Wallace Progressive white, black 2 in. pin evokes memory of FDR.

Collector's Choice—George Wallace, American Independent Nominee, 1968

"Wallace Send Them a Message"; word pin w, blk. $1^1/_4$ in.

"Win with Wallace," Liberty Bell symbol w, blk; $1^1/_4$ in.

"Wallace School Bus" cartoon of Wallace leaning on front of bus: b, w, blk, o; $1^1/_2$ in.

47th Election–1972

President: Richard M. Nixon (R)
Vice-President: Spiro T. Agnew (replaced by Gerald Ford and later, Nelson Rockefeller)
Defeated candidates:
George McGovern (D) and Thomas Eagleton (replaced by R. Sargent Shriver)
John G. Schmitz (A)
Linda Jenness (SW)
A relative unknown, Senator George McGovern of South Dakota, had emerged after 1971 as the leading spokesman for a variety of protest groups, including anti-Vietnam activists, ERA and black civil righters. McGovern as Democrat's nominee called for immediate withdrawal of US troops from Vietnam, plus amnesty for those who refused to serve their country in that war. Abolishing capital punishment, banning handgun sales and advocating free choice as to life styles and sexual preferences were all major Democrat platform considerations.

Missouri Senator Thomas Eagleton, a Catholic liberal, seemed a popular choice as McGovern's running mate. Then came the unsettling news that Eagleton had suffered severe depression on several occasions in the past, requiring hospitalization and electric-shock treatment. McGovern insisted on keeping Eagleton on the ticket, backing him "1,000 percent." But heavy pressure from his advisers led him to do an about-face and Eagleton was asked to withdraw from the race. After a frantic search, the Democrats turned to R. Sargent Shriver, of Illinois, former Peace Corps director, ambassador to France and a JFK brother-in-law. Despite the damage control, by waffling during the Eagleton crisis, McGovern's credibility grew clearly suspect.

Nixon's renomination was more like a coronation. During the '72 campaign, he removed himself from the infighting, burnishing his image as world leader while sending Spiro Agnew and staff on the campaign trail.

In an outright debacle, some 78 million voted to give Nixon a huge popular plurality approaching 18,000,000 votes. Winning the election by 60.7 percent, 47,165,234 to 29,168,110. In the electoral count, the GOP totaled 520 vs. 17 (though one Virginia elector withheld his vote). McGovern carried only Massachusetts and the District of Columbia.

The Republican story did not have a happy ending. On October 1973, Spiro Agnew, charged with income tax evasion, was forced out of office. Nixon replaced him with Gerald Ford of Michigan. Then came the Watergate break-in and a sorry litany of intimidation, forgery, sabotage, bribery and perjury led to the indictment of 20 members of Nixon's administration and a trail that led directly to the Oval Office. Facing impeachment, Nixon resigned as president on August 8, 1974. Gerald Ford, who stepped into Nixon's shoes after Watergate, had the dubious distinction of becoming the first chief executive who had been appointed, but not elected either as president or as vice president.

Collector's Choice—George McGovern, Democratic Nominee, 1972

"Come Home America/McGovern/Shriver" jugate; r, w, b, blk, 1972; 1³/4 in.

"For Peace/McGovern" cartoon of standing McGovern holding dove with peace branch in bill; b, w, blk; 2 in.

"Fox Valley, Ill/McGovern" 1972 cartoon head of Fox paired with McGovern; r, y, blk; 2¹/4 in.

"McGovern/For Our Children" idyllic scene of child amid flowers with cloud b, g; pop art beauty; multicolor in oval padded cloth on tin; 2³/4 in.

"George McGovern . . . for President . . . now!" picture button with psychedelic flag and pair of silhouetted doves; r, w, b, blk; 3 in.

"George McGovern is the Real Eugene McCarthy" slogan button attempts to link McCarthy to Eugene McCarthy's peace platform; b, w; 1¹/2 in.

"Make Something Happen Again/McGovern" stylized trees and mountains; b, gr, w, blk; 1¹/2 in.

"McGovern-Eagleton" 1972 one of two slogan pins known issued before Eagleton's withdrawal.

"McGovern" Rainbow, multicolor; 1¹/2 in.

"Vote for McGovern" 1972 Peter Max design of op art face/sunburst; b, gr, br, w; 1¹/2 in.

"Robin McGovern" 1972 smiling McGovern picture button in Robin Hood regalia; b, w, g' 4 in.

"Vote for McGovern/Shriver" jugate of smiling Democrat nominees; w, blk; 1¹/4 in.

48ᵗʰ Election—1976

President: James E. Carter (D)
Vice President: Walter Mondale
Defeated candidates:
Gerald Ford (R) and Robert Dole
Eugene McCarthy (I)
Roger Macbride (L)
Lester Maddox (AI)

While George McGovern failed to tap the support of mainstream America, Jimmy Carter, another outsider and a former governor of Georgia who was vastly inexperienced in political infighting on Capitol Hill, somehow found the magic formula. Carter, a US Naval Academy graduate, served as a nuclear sub commander in the Navy under Admiral Hyman Rickover.

For two years prior to the election, Carter relentlessly crisscrossed the country, pressing the flesh and declaring in his Georgian drawl, "My name is Jimmy Carter and I'm running for President."

Incumbent Gerry Ford, who filled in when Nixon resigned, had to stave off a bid at the Republican convention by movie idol and two-term Governor of California, Ronald Reagan to clinch the nomination. Ford's running mate was Kansas senator Bob Dole, a seasoned, skilled politician.

In the second of the greatly-hyped series of TV debates during the campaign, Ford fumbled a question by denying the Soviet domination in Eastern Europe, thus creating the impression of being mistake-prone, a perception from which he never fully recovered.

Carter, a born-again Christian, also had his cross to bear. His ill-advised *Playboy* interview and comment on lust made headlines and caused great merriment in the Ford camp.

In November, the voters gave Carter 297 electoral votes to Ford's 240 and a margin of victory of almost 1,700,000 votes with 40,828,587 to 39,147,613.

Eugene McCarthy, an Independent, picked up 751,728 and the American Independent's white supremacist Governor Lester Maddox of Georgia tallied 170,780.

Collector's Choice—39th President James E. Carter

Carter's buttons usually follow a green and white color scheme, a combination that he chose early on in his race for governor in 1971.

"I Am for Alabama COPE" scarce jugate Carter–Mondale; g, w, blk; 1³/4 in.

"America's Third Century/Why Not the Best?" Carter-Mondale jugate; w, g, blk; 1³/4 in.

"Carter Works for Peanuts" cluster of three unshelled peanuts; blk, tan; $1^3/4$ in.

"My name is Jimmy Carter and I'm running for president." Carter picture button; $1^1/4$ in.

Carter in his favorite green and white color scheme is extolled as "A Leader For a Change"

"Carter Is Smarter" slogan button; white reverse out of green: $2^1/4$ in.

"Grits and Fritz in '76" name pin green, w; 2 in.

"I'm a Bunny for Carter" with name stylized to form a rabbit, inspired by *Playboy* interview; br, blk, w; $2^1/8$ in.

"The Coming of Carter" classic cartoon of Carter in straw hat as peanut farmer; multicolor; $2^1/4$ in.

"Jimmy Carter-Walter Mondale" photo flasher button; w, blk; 2 in.

"The South Has Risen" cartoon of Carter peanut waving Confederate flag; green, w; $1^3/4$ in.

Collector's Choice—Anti- Carter

"Do You Want A Nut In The White House" cartoon of Mr. Peanut with cane and top hat; br, blk, w; 3 in.

"Lust with Carter/Win with Ford" slogan button; reverse white out of black; $1^1/4$ in.

"Peanut Power" giant peanut caricature of Carter eating GOP elephant; g, w; $2^1/8$ in.

"Carter-Mondale" jugate salesmen's sample pin by Phillips Co. (uncirculated prototype); stars and stripes; b, g, r, w, blk.

Collector's Choice—Gerald Ford
GOP Nominee, 1976

(Rebus of Model T Ford) For President" 1976; r, w, b, blk; 3 in.

"Ford" cartoon of elephant as a boxer putting up his dukes; g, w, blk; $2^1/4$ in.

"Ford–Dole-Steelman" (Alan Steelman of Texas) completes this cartoon of GOP elephant "putting the boot" to Democrat donkey; r, w, b; $1^1/2$ in.

Gerald Ford "no name rebus button; red, white, blue, black, 2 in.

Jimmy Carter gives lift to Gerald Ford in '76.

"Shootout at Kansas City/Republican National Convention/1976/I Was There"; cartoon version of High Noon; cowboys Ford in white hat and Reagan in black hat; Ford won the nomination; w, blk; 7 in. showpiece.

"Jerry Ford for Congress" name pin from one of Ford's congressional runs; r, w, b; 2¼ in.

Collector's Choice—Anti-Ford

"Ford Is An Edsel" word pin; w, blk; 2 in.

"Jerry" stylized full image of Jerry Ford on the go with briefcase; r, w, blk; 1⅛ In.

"Trade in Your Ford in '76" cartoon of Edsel with Jerry as hood ornament; Capitol in b, g, r, w, b; 2 ½ in.

49th Election—1980

President: Ronald Reagan (R)
Vice President: George H. W. Bush
Defeated candidates:
James E. Carter (D) and Walter Mondale
John Anderson (I) and Patrick Lucey

Ronald Reagan was able to turn the war-or-peace issue against Carter, charging that the incumbent's weakness in allowing our allies to no longer respect us, posed "a far greater danger of unwanted inadvertent war." Reagan's stance was that America build up its defense capability to the point that the country can keep the peace.

Reagan's experience as a former film, radio and TV performer gave him an edge while stumping for the presidency and he was a master of timing. Even so, he had his gaffes: Reagan stated he favored restoring official relations with Taiwan, infuriating China even as George

H. W. Bush, his running mate, was in Peking on a good-will tour. Reagan blamed trees, not automobiles for smog and announced that air pollution had been "substantially controlled." Shortly afterward, his plane was delayed because Los Angeles suffered one of its worst smog attacks in years.

The GOP made much of Jimmy Carter's "Billygate" (a word play on Nixon's Watergate), a revelation that his precocious brother Billy had accepted $220,000 from the Libyan government for lobbying efforts in the U.S. After a Congressional probe, Billy eventually later defused the issue by admitting "bad judgment" and registered as an agent of a foreign power. This prompted Reagan supporter Bob Hope's quip, "the difference between Jimmy and his brother, was that "Billy had a foreign policy."

In the final analysis, the Great Inflation and the failure to secure the release of American hostages in Iran did Carter in. It was the most stunning defeat for a presidential incumbent since Hoover's loss to FDR almost a half-century earlier. Reagan's popular plurality was 8,300,000 votes, 10 percent of the total. He garnered 43,899,248 votes, 51 percent. He took 489 electoral votes to Carter's 49, losing only Georgia, Minnesota, West Virginia, Rhode Island, Hawaii and the District of Columbia.

Almost overlooked was John B. Anderson's bid for the brass ring. The popular Illinois congressman, running on the Independent ticket, won 5,719,437 votes.

Reagan was 69 when he entered the White House, the oldest president in history, topping William Henry Harrison.

Collector's Choice—40th President
Ronald Reagan

A variety of 1980s Reagan buttons portrayed him wearing a Stetson as a virile cowboy:

"Reagan '80" bust photo in big white cowboy hat; multicolor; $1^1/4$ in.

Reagan-John Wayne jugate no-name with Dutch and Duke dressed in cowboy duds; w, blk; $1^1/4$ in.

"Ronald Reagan 1960/Right to Bear Arms" large eagle and US shield; light blue, blk; $2^1/4$ in.

1980 Ronald Reagan takeoff on TV show *Dallas;* white, black; 4 in.

"Working Man's Candidate/Citizens for Reagan '80" silhouette of a hard hat; calls attention to fundamental political realignment his candidacy had created.

Collector's Choice—Anti-Reagan

"He Ain't Headin' West! This Is Not a Movie" cartoon classic of GOP elephant atop hill watching as wagon train rolls by; multicolor; rectangle; $2^3/4$ in. h.

"Stop Pollution/Nuke the Trees" refers to Reagan's celebrated gaffe that trees generate more pollution than cars.

"Reagan-Bush/That's All Folks" cartoon of mushroom cloud; y, blk; $1^3/4$ in.

"Reagan/The Fascist Gun in the West" Student Democrats in Minnesota issue.

"El Salvador is Reagan's War On Poverty."

"Robin Hood/Rob from the Poor/Give to the Rich" Reagan bust in Robin Hood attire; gld, tan, w; $1^3/4$ in.

"Protect Pro-Life for Reagan"; New Jersey Pro Life Pac issue, showing a pair of fetuses in tiny ovals.

"The Bayou State/Reagan Country/Ours After 102 Years/Louisiana 1980" unusual design of Baton Rouge skyscraper; b, w; 4 in.

Collector's Choice—Reagan–Bush Jugates

Reagan-Bush/Lets Make America Great Again" 1980 jugate of smiling candidates, encircled with tiny GOP elephants; r, w, b, blk; 3 in. showpiece .

"America Loves Reagan-Bush/1984" conjoining portraits in heart shape; w, r, w, b, blk; 2 in. h. x $1^1/2$ in.

"Bringing America Back/Reagan-Bush" r, w, b, blk; $1^1/2$ in. h. x 2 in. w.

"Help Keep America Great/Re-elect Ronald Reagan," flag background; r, w, b, blk; $1^1/4$ in.

"Reagan-Bush" eagle over portraits, flag, shield; r, w, b, blk; 1 in.

Reagan-Bush no-name, striped shield between oval portraits; r, w, b, blk; 1 in.

"Reagan-Bush One More Time"

50th Election—1984

President: Ronald Reagan (R)
Vice President: George H.W. Bush
Defeated candidates:
Walter Mondale (D) and Geraldine Ferraro
David Bergland (L)
Lyndon LaRouche (I)

The significant breakthrough in the '84 race was the inclusion of Geraldine Ferraro as running mate to Walter Mondale. New Jersey Congresswoman Ferraro became the first female to appear on the national ticket of a major political party.

Ronald Reagan had done more to re-engineer the basic scope and substance of national government in his own image than any other American over the last half century. The incumbent 1984 agenda was far less unencumbered by conservative slogans, symbols and themes than his previous run for high office.

After Geraldine Ferraro had joined the Democratic ticket, the GOP strategy was to project a clearly-articulated message to convince American women, who were swarming to the polls in increasing numbers, to vote for Reagan—this despite Reagan's hawkish first term and his opposition to affirmative action quotas, ratification of ERA and other feminist objectives. Especially active in helping to woo the women's vote was the American Women Supporting the President. A colorful cartoon button "Women for Reagan-Bush '84" depicts an elephant attired in a flower decorated hat and a ribbon on its tail. Reagan clearly benefited from an outpouring of more women-oriented campaign items than any other candidate in history.

With disclosure of irregularities in Ferraro's campaign contributions FECA reports ("Come Clean Geraldine" read one of the cryptic buttons), and scandal of kickbacks on the part by her husband, contractor John Zaccaro, the Democrats sorely needed damage control.

A number of strident feminist groups served the ticket shabbily by demeaning Mondale as they exalted Ferraro e.g., a vendor button shows Ferraro walking Mondale as an obedient dog on a leash, inscribed "Hurry Up Fritz" and a slogan button reading "Ferraro and What's His Name."

It was no contest as Reagan rampaged to the highest electoral total in history at 525 vs. 13 as Mondale won only his home state of Minnesota and the District of Columbia. The popular vote ran 54,450,603 to 37,573,671. Libertarian David Bergland tallied 227,949 votes and a new arrival on the scene, Independent Lyndon LaRouche managed 78,773.

Collector's Choice—40th President
Ronald Reagan
Anti-Reagan

Democrats on the attack against Reagan inspired more hostile campaign items than for any candidate since Willkie's blast from the past vented at FDR's in his third term run in 1940.

Tops among an extraordinary array of buttons were such slogan entries as: "Dump Reagan," a convention caricature piece picturing Reagan upside-down in a trash can, titled "Impeach The Leech/Put The Button Out Of his Reach" implying that a hawkish Reagan was trigger-happy.

"California Home of Mickey Mouse and Ronald Reagan/Mickey For Pres!" map of California; w, blk; 2^1/4 in.

"Do Nothing Cal Coolidge/Depression Hero Herbert Hoover/Recession Ronnie Reagan" slogan button; g, w; 1^3/4 in.

"Let Them Eat Jelly Beans." (Links Reagan's fondness for jelly beans and takeoff on Marie Antoinette's famed rejoinder.)

"Jane Wyman was Right" snide referral to Reagan's unsuccessful first marriage.

"Bonzo Goes to Washington" alludes to Reagan's film with chimp, *Bedtime For Bonzo*.

A Democratic Women Power entry features snarling bulldog and legend "Gr-r-r." translates as "Get Rid of Ronald Reagan."

On one occasion during a speech, while testing a micro-phone, Ronald Reagan made a joke about bombing the Soviets, prompting a pin picturing a laughing president with mushroom cloud in b, g, worded "We begin bombing in five minutes."

"Reagan Gnu" a caricature button of a gnu with Reagan's head projecting from its backside, relates to the Iran-Contra Affair when word leaked out that Iran allegedly purchased American arms as part of the deal to release American hostages (Reagan denied knowledge of this deal).

"Throw the Bums Out," cartoon of hand with thumb shaped like a dove giving umpire's "out" sign; disembodied head of Reagan; b, w, blk; $2^1/4$ in.

Pro-Reagan

"In Reagan We Trust" Portrait of Reagan as if pictured on paper currency; g, blk; $2^1/4$ in.

"Let's Make America Great Again" Reagan bust photo flasher pin; b, w, blk: $2^1/2$ in.

"Mississippi Women Love Reagan/Vote Reagan '96" Southern belles salute Reagan with photo button against hearts and stars; g, r, w, b; $1^3/4$ in.

"Re-elect Reagan in '84/Deal Me In" Reagan picture superimposed on Ace of Hearts card; r, w, b; $1^3/4$ in. h.

"Ronnie's Angels" cartoon of angel wearing halo; w, blk; $1^3/4$ in.

"Vermont/Reagan Country" scarce slogan pin with stylized snowflake pattern; b, w; $1^3/4$ in.

Collector's Choice—Walter Mondale, Democratic Nominee, 1984

"A Women's Place is in the House/In the Senate & Vice Presidency/Ferraro '84."

"Be Emphatic/Vote Straight Democratic" head photos of Mondale, Ferraro and Michigan coattail candidates; r, w, b; $1^3/4$ in.

"Democrat's Care About America/Mondale-Ferraro" jugate (note incorrect plural of word 'Democrat'; b, w; $2^1/8$ in.

1984 Walter Mondale–Geraldine Ferraro 1¼ in.; red, white, blue, black. (50th Election).

"Ferraro-Mondale" jugate in which larger image of Ferraro upstages small Mondale image in b.g.; r, w, b, blk; 1¾ in.;

"First Americans for Mondale" slogan oval; one of the few examples of a Native American endorsement; r, w, b; 1¾ in.

"Geraldine Ferraro/America's First Woman " '84 portrait button; r, w, b, blk, w; 3½ in.

"Fritz-Busters" cartoon of Mondale with overprinted with a red bar; takeoff on "Ghostbusters"; r, w, blk; 2¼ in.

"Mondale-Ferraro" bleed-off jugate photo of the pair waving; r, w, blk; 1¾ in.

"Now! 1984" Portrait button of Ferraro; r, w, b, blk; 1¾ in.

"SWIA Supports Mondale-Ferraro" photo of Mondale and Ferraro waving; Machinist Labor union issue; r, w, b; 1¾ in.

51st Election—1988

President: George H. W. Bush (R)
Vice President: Dan Quayle
Defeated candidates:
Michael Dukakis (D) and Lloyd Bentsen, Jr.

George H.W. Bush, Reagan's vice president in the previous two terms, faced a number of challenges on the eve of the 1988 race. His immediate problem focused on his role in the Iran-Contra scandal, an issue that refused to go away. Bush's live interview with Dan Rather of *CBS News* in January, in which Bush bristled and stood up well under Rather's aggressive prodding, helped erase his preppy, wimp image with the still suspicious conservative wing of the GOP. Bush's hardball tactics in the primaries paid off against a formidable opponent, Robert Dole of Kansas. Bush attacked Dole's votes for tax increases in the Senate. A few weeks later, on Super Tuesday in the South, Bush posted solid wins in all the southern states and put Dole's candidacy on the ropes.

The Democrats nominated a moderate centrist, Governor Michael Dukakis of Massachusetts, for the top post and opinion polls quickly gave the governor a lead as high as sixteen points over Bush. Senator Lloyd M. Bentsen Jr., of Texas, who had beaten Bush in a senatorial race in 1970, was the vice-presidential nominee.

Bush's rousing acceptance speech at the GOP convention in New Orleans voiced a promise that would propel him to victory in 1988. Bush assailed Dukakis for having vetoed as governor a bill requiring school children to recite the Pledge of Allegiance. He resonated a recurring campaign theme championing private charities as "a brilliant diversity spread like stars, like a thousand points of light in a broad and peaceful sky." Then, borrowing a line from movie gunslinger Clint Eastwood, he stated, that Congress would push and push him to raise taxes but his answer: "Read my lips. No new Taxes!"

J. Danforth "Dan" Quayle, a young second-term senator from Indiana was nominated as Bush's running mate.

Many observers believe Michael Dukakis lost the election when a barrage of TV commercials dredged up the Willie Horton furlough incident. As governor, Dukakis had continued a policy of granting weekend furloughs to convicts. Willie Horton, an African-American serving a life sentence for murder, when released on furlough, fled to Maryland where he assaulted a couple, raping the woman. The Democrats failed to counter that Ronald Reagan had pursued a similar arrangement while governor of California.

Bush seemed to "one-up" Dukakis in the televised debates, particularly when the Democrat came off as cold and unfeeling in response to a hypothetical question, "would he endorse the death penalty if someone raped his own, wife, Kitty Dukakis?"

The Bush victory was overwhelming with 426 electoral votes vs. Dukakis 111; Bush's popular vote total was 48,881,221 and Dukakis won 41,805,422.

Collector's Choice—41st President George Bush

"The Best Woman for this Job Is a Man" George Bush vice-presidential slogan button put-down of Bush's vice-presidential opponent Geraldine Ferraro in 1984; w, blk; 2 in.

"Bush–Dole+'88" female symbol on slogan pin boosts Elizabeth Dole as running mate; $1^1/4$ in.

"Bush–Quayle '92 Republican National Convention/ Pennsylvania Delegation in Houston/No. 175"; r, w, b; (scarce numbered pin.); 4 in.

1988 Bush Quayle/GOP Elephant Ears jugate: r, blk, w; 2 in.

"The Rise to the Top" George Bush, Dan Quayle & Ohio coattail; trigate photo of candidates inside a cartoon blimp. Unusual oval, r, w, b, blk and gld; $2^1/2$ in.

"Bush–Quayle Pennsylvania Delegation/'92/Republican National Convention/Houston"; prize delegation numbered pin; line portraits of pair with flag; r, w, b; 4 in.

"George Bush Would Make a Very Decent President I Must Say"; cartoon of Bush in front of White House.

"Torpedo Bomber Bush for President/Veterans for Bush '80"; Bush pictured with Navy Bomber in b.g. oval; pin; b,w; $2^1/2$ in.

Two of the most creative rebus buttons in the modern era, were $7/8$ in. b, w images of an large bush and a quail (read: Bush-Quayle).

Collector's Choice—Anti-Quayle

Quayle "This Spuds On You," anti-Bush cartoon pin shows Vice President Quayle in dunce cap marked "Quayle Mr. Potato"; refers to his stumbling on word "potato" in a much publicized spelling bee; w, blk; 2 in.

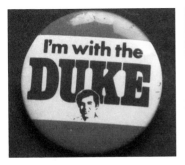

"We Are The Most Powerful Planet on Earth—Quayle;" word pin; another Dem swipe at Quayle's foot-in-mouth propensity; w, b; 1¹/4 in.

Collector's Choice—Michael Dukakis–Lloyd Bentsen

"Aiming for a Lower Debt & Balance of Payments"; cartoon of Dukakis aiming at a bush and quail rebus figures; multicolor; 1³/4 in.

"Alaska for Dukakis/Bentsen 1988"; r, w, b; 2¹/4 in.

"A New Beginning in '88/Dukakis-Bentsen"; r, w, b, blk; 1³/4 in.

"Dukakis/1988/Bentsen" jugate flanks White House illustration; multicolor; 6 in.

"Dukakis-Jesse Jackson/1988," jugate portrait; pre-convention of a possible slate; r, w, b, blk; 2¹/4 in.

"South Dakotas for Dukakis," showing the Presidents on Mount Rushmore in b.g.; r, w, b, Rates as one of the top state party issues; 2¹/4 in.

An anti-Dukakis vendor button shows the governor looking rather ridiculous posing with his head sticking out of a turret of an army tank in full camouflage mufti.

1988 Mike Dukakis buttons; cartoon example at right was issued by New Hampshire Young Republicans during the primaries; red, black, white; 1¹/4 in.

52nd Election—1992

President: Bill Clinton (D)
Vice President: Al Gore
Defeated candidates:
George Bush (R) and Dan Quayle
H. Ross Perot (I)

George Bush's commendable four years in office were highlighted by sending troops to Panama to capture

1992 George Bush-Dan Quayle 2¹/₄ in. (51st election).

strongman Manuel Noriega, adroitly managing the fallout from the USSR collapse; and the Gulf War triumph. Domestically, the Americans with Disabilities Act and the resolution of the savings and loan scandal inherited from Reagan were feathers in his cap.

The quandary confronting Bush was the issue of taxes. In June of 1990, the President announced that dealing with the deficit might require "tax revenue increases," breaking his 1988 pledge. Bush negotiators struck a deal with the Democrats with a deficit reduction package proposed to raise the highest marginal tax rate, to be offset with cuts in proposed increases in the gasoline tax. This infuriated Republicans in the House and Senate as three-quarters of those members voted against the administration.

At first Iraq's invasion of Kuwait and a US victory in the Gulf War took the country's mind off taxes and Bush's boost in the popularity polls gave him little incentive to broaden his GOP base. A brief, acute recession, the first in eight years, aroused fears among the populace as Americans who feared that the benefits of Social Security and Medicare would be unavailable for them in their retirement years.

Despite a twenty-point dip in his job approval rating in early fall of 1991, Bush failed to articulate a vision or direction to take the nation. Vice President Quayle later agonized, "This was the most poorly planned and executed incumbent presidential campaign in this century."

In Spring 1992, Arkansas Governor William Jefferson Clinton announced his Democratic candidacy. Clinton however, beset by personal problems, including marital infidelity, was dismissed as a serious threat to Bush's run. Albert Gore, a Senator from Tennessee was picked as Clinton's running mate.

In the campaign's early stages, several splinter-party candidates succeeded in enlivening the race. Former

Nixon and Reagan aide Patrick "Pat" Buchanan left his cable TV political show for the campaign trail. Bush bested Buchanan in the New Hampshire Primary; but Buchanan's promises of reviving the moribund state of the economy resonated with voters. Swing voters were highly intrigued with Ross Perot, a feisty Texas billionaire whose TV commercials included pie-charts and hard-talking rhetoric. On the eve of the Democratic convention, Perot abruptly dropped out of the picture, but then re-entered the race in October, further hurting Bush's chances.

Though Bush was undoubtedly done in by the economy, many observers felt the death knell sounded just five days before election. Lawrence Walsh, the Independent counsel investigating Iran-Contra, indicted Reagan Secretary of Defense Caspar Weinberger, and court documents filed contained information implicating Bush as having knowledge of the plot to exchange arms for hostages, a charge Bush had vehemently denied.

The GOP defeat proved devastating. Clinton won 370 votes to 168 for Bush. The popular vote ran Clinton: 44,908,254 (43 percent); Bush 39,102,343 (37 percent). Independent Ross Perot (19 percent), shut out in that category, Perot polled 19,741,065 popular votes.

Collector's Choice—42nd President
William Jefferson Clinton

"An American Reunion/The 53rd Presidential Inauguration Gala"; r, w, b; Clinton playing saxophone, cameo shots of Barbra Streisand, Elton John and other singing stars, 3 in.

"A New Covenant /Hope For America" Clinton profile against b.g. of Statue of Liberty; multicolor; 2¹/4 in.

"Cure for the Blues" Clinton in dark glasses playing saxophone; w, blk; 2 in.

Clinton-Dole, no-name vertical oval jugate with portraits inside stylized "96"; b, w, blk numerals; 2 in.

"Immanuel Baptist Church Choir & Orchestra Inaugural Participation in '97"; portrait bust of Clinton, identifying him as member of the choir; r, w, b, blk; 3¹/2 in.

1996 Grateful Dead 2¼ in. red, white, blue, black put Bill Clinton and Al Gore on "Glory Road."

Sesame Street PBS Bill Clinton–Al Gore (53rd election).

"Our Native Son/Clinton For President/'92" name pin with map of Arkansas; r, w, b; 2 in.

"Rock-n-Roll with Clinton/Cleveland, Ohio"; slogan pin; r, w, b; 2 in.

"Regain Democracy/Clinton" Clinton and Gore as joggers; vendor favorite; multicolor; 2 in.

"Stop the Church Burning/African Americans for Clinton-Gore '96" slogan button; w, blk; 1¾ in.

Collector's Choice—Anti-Clinton

"He just keeps on lying . . . " cartoon of Clinton as Ever Ready Bunny; r, w, b; 2 in.

"Inhale to the Chief" photo of young Clinton with smoking joint; choice vendor pin; w, blk; 2 in.

"The Pride of the Gay and Lesbian Community" Clinton portrait horiz. oval; r, w, b; 2¼ in.

Collector's Choice—Anti-Bush

"Annoy The Media/Re-elect Bush"; photo of Bush holding up one of his one bumper stickers; multicolor; 1¾ in.

"Who's Sane?" cartoon of Bush waving flag; top armored tank; anti-Gulf War; r, w, b; 2¼ in.

53rd Election 1996

President: Bill Clinton(D)
Vice President: Al Gore
Defeated candidates:
Bob Dole (R)
and Jack Kemp
Incumbent President Bill Clinton had run and won as a Centrist Democrat. A strong partisan infighter, Clinton,

the first baby-boomer president, typified everything the GOP and Christian Right abhorred: self-indulgence, infidelity and behaving like a modern-day JFK in his sexual dalliances.

The first two years gave the GOP high hopes of a shoo-in win in 1996 with Clinton's endorsement of gays in the military and his Attorney General Janet Reno's mishandling of the incendiary Branch Davidian episode in Waco, Texas in April 1993. A convoluted and costly health care program endorsed by First Lady Hillary Clinton had become an embarrassment for the Democrats.

The real crusher was the tax increase the Democrats pushed through Congress later that summer. The GOP's Newt Gingrich of Georgia, who had achieved the unthinkable—winning a majority in the House and making himself majority Speaker, forecast "a job-killing recession," when the bill passed.

Then the political landscape changed, as it so often happens in our history. The horrific terrorist bombing of the US Federal Building in Oklahoma City on April 19, 1995, President Clinton's moving memorial tribute to the 160 victims, and personal contact with the bereaved families, clearly burnished his leadership image.

Unable to get a budget agreement with the Democrats, two government shut-downs resulted at the end of 1995 and the GOP was blamed for the stalemate. As that perception persisted, GOP Congressional leaders agreed to reopen the government in January 1996.

The Republicans had hoped to coax Gulf War hero Gen. Colin Powell to run for president, but the General remained noncommittal. Senator Bob Dole, now 72, had lost an early race in New Hampshire to Pat Buchanan and faced a formidable challenger in millionaire publisher Steve Forbes. Dole fared well in the Southern primaries to win the nomination, but ran also woefully shy of campaign funds.

At the GOP convention Dole startled the delegates by proposing a fifteen percent tax cut over a three-year period that would produce a "fairer, flatter tax." Dole selected as his running mate former congressman Jack

1996 Bob Dole cyclone wreaks havoc on Democratic donkeys in red, white, blue black 3-in. (53rd election).

Kemp of New York, a former Buffalo Bills star quarterback was a big advocate of tax cuts. He proved less productive in gaining votes than he had in scoring NFL touchdowns.

By mid-October, with Clinton coasting with a double digit lead, revelations surfaced that Clinton had received campaign contributions from business interests in the Far East, possibly involving Communist Chinese and Indonesian factions. As the Clinton lead narrowed, Dole made a last-ditch whirlwind tour of the country to try to close the gap, but it was not to happen.

Clinton's successful bid for a second term, was nearly a carbon copy of his winning margins in 1992. He won 47,401,185 popular votes to Dole's 39,197,469; electorally it was Clinton 379, Dole 159. Perot, running on the Reform ticket, dropped to 8,085,294 less than half his total in 1992.

Collector's Choice—Bob Dole

"Dole-Kemp/'96" jugate of Dole-Kemp with large pineapple in b.g; multicolor; 3 in.

"Victory '96 Party/Nov. 5, 1996/GOP"; cartoon of elephant head with jugate images of Dole-Kemp appeared inside elephant's ears (reminiscent of the Taft 1904 classic); multicolor: 2 in.

"Louisville Welcomes Bob Dole/1996" Dole bust picture pin with map of Kentucky; r, w, b; 1³/4 in.

"'96 Bob Dole/Illinois/Al Salvi/'96" coattail name button; r, w, b; 1³/4 in.

"Bob Dole For President/Taxes, Taxes, Taxes Help!" Dole portrait; multicolor; 1³/4 in.

"Touchdown in Washington" Bob Dole-Jack Kemp bust photos inside large football; multicolor; 1³/4 in.

Collector's Choice—Anti-Dole

"Butt Heads For Bob" cartoon of three dancing cigarette butts; r, w, b, blk; 1³/4 in.

54th Election—2000

President: George W. Bush (R)
Vice President: Dick Cheney
Defeated candidates: Al Gore (D) and Joseph Lieberman

Countdown to the 2000 Race

The GOP went for the jugular in autumn of 1998, pursuing the Clinton–Lewinsky scandal with disseminated reports by independent counsel Kenneth Starr making the case for Clinton's impeachment. This strategy backfired as the partisanship of the GOP infuriated the Democrats, who in a stunning backlash, gained five seats in the House and cut the GOP majority 221-211. The upsets sealed the fate of Newt Gingrich, who elected to step down after sensing that chances of his re-election as House Speaker, were in jeopardy.

On December 19, 1998, President Clinton, was impeached by the House of Representatives in connection with a cover-up in a relationship with a former White House intern, Monica Lewinsky. He was tried in the Senate in 1999 and subsequently acquitted.

In *Grand Old Party* Lewis Gould writes that in the end, the GOP "did not have sufficient determination to put aside partisanship and reach out to Democrats . . . and had trivialized impeachment as a meaningless constitutional weapon."

The GOP presidential field was again a crowded one in 2000, but two candidates clearly seemed to have the inside track. George W. Bush, son of George H. W. Bush, in 1998 had dismantled a weak Democratic slate to win his second term as governor of Texas.

Bush's main challenge came from Senator John McCain of Arizona, with a heroic war record with a reputation as a maverick who shot from the hip. Infuriated by the corrupting flow of money into American politics, McCain with Sen. Russell Feinstein, a Wisconsin Democrat, led the fight for campaign finance reform. McCain pulled an upset over Bush in the New Hampshire primary with a decisive win. While McCain performed well in primaries where independents could vote, Bush's strong campaign organization and a war chest of $100 million going into the primaries had the race locked up by the spring of 2000. He immediately proposed as his main thrust, a $1.6 trillion tax cut, to take effect over a ten-year period. In addition to his radical tax cut proposal, Bush took a "risky" course by proposing that workers be allowed to invest portions of Social Security payroll contributions in private accounts to take advantage of future gains in the stock market—a smokescreen for his real goal, to make Social Security a completely voluntary system.

In one of the debates, Bush was on record as opposing a supervisory foreign policy for the US over other countries, "I'm not so sure our role is to go around the world saying this is the way its got to be" (articulating the GOP's unease with Democratic military commitments and other trouble spots). Less than a year into his presidency, Bush did an about-face with a containment policy backed by military actions in Afghanistan and Iraq.

Bush's choice for a running mate was Richard "Dick" Cheney of Wyoming, an avowed conservative and the CEO of Halliburton Industries.

When Clinton's vice president, Al Gore, breezed in easily to get the presidential nomination at the Democratic convention, his party assumed an early lead in the polls. Joe Lieberman, a seasoned senator from Connecticut, received the nod as the vice presidential nominee.

The three highly-touted televised debates between Gore-Bush proved a "wash" as both candidates performed as if in a trance, despite Gore's edge as a seasoned debater.

The Democrats again dredged up rumors about Bush's alcohol abuse and drug use as a young man, citing a drunken-driving conviction twenty-five years earlier; and reminding voters that his military record as a National Guardsman in the early 1970s had unexplained gaps. In the final analysis, the legacy of the Clinton scandals dogged Gore. So, too, did his lack of rapport with the national press corps who considered him a bit of a stuffed shirt and privately rooted for his defeat.

Election Day 2000 proved to be nothing short of calamitous.

Gore enjoyed a 540,000 plurality in the popular vote (51,003,894 to 50,459,211) and had won, or was ahead with 266 electoral votes to Bush's 246. The TV networks prematurely placed Florida's decisive 25 electoral votes in Gore's column, but then re-tracted and called it for Bush, fi-nally deeming it too close to call. Gore's forces charged that ballot irregularities and errors in the Florida count deprived him of the votes needed to put the Democrats over the top.

Thus was waged the so-called "Battle of the Chads" with law-suits, court proceedings and recounts dominating the head-lines throughout November and December. The dispute reached the US Supreme Court in December and the justices ruled 5-4 in *Bush vs. Gore* that the Florida vote recorded by George W's brother, Governor Jeb Bush, should be final.

2000 G.W. Bush –Harry Potter jugate; red, white, blue and black; 2 in.

The revised electoral count: Bush 271; Gore 266. Many observers felt that the 2,834,410 votes siphoned off by Green party candidate Ralph Nader cost the Democrats dearly. Gore accepted the decision and George Bush emerged as president-elect.

Collector's Choice—43rd President George W. Bush

1990 Texas Governor's Race

"Brazos County /Rep. Party Bush For Texas Governor/ Volunteer" slogan button; r, w; 2 in.

"George Jr./Governor TX. '90; First Bush Texas Gov." pin; r, w; 2 in. 1996

2000 Presidential Race

"American"; multicolor; 1¼ in.

"Bulldogs for Bush/2004" photo of bulldog against large Y for Yale b.g.; w, b, blk; 2 in.

Bush-Cheney "Elephant Ears" jugate oval portraits in elephant ear's design; r, gld., blk, 2⅛ in.

"Dubya/Dubya/Dubya/on ebay.com": r, w, b; 3 in.

"Hit a Home Run for America" Bush's head supered on large baseball; multicolor; 3 in.

2000 G. W. Bush–Al Gore Florida recount mechanical spinner button and Butterfly Chad Bush-Gore pins; multicolor.

"Put Bush Back on the 'Right Road'/Bush-Cheney 2000;" jugate insets appear inside Road "66" in Republican shield in black silhouette; b, w, blk; 6 in.

"From Washington D.C. to Jefferson City /Missouri Values" 2000 numerals picture Bush, and five Missouri office-seekers, pin includes John Ashcroft, who lost his senatorial race, but later became attorney general; b, blk, w; $3^1/2$ in.

"George W. Bush and the Environment/Nevada"; Bush-Cheney jugates flanking photo of buffalo on range; multicolor; 6 in.

"I Voted for W/Bush-Cheney" Large "W" in stars and stripes design; r, w, b; 2 in.

"Republican Candidates/2000" Bush Cheney jugates, multicolor; 2 in.

"Super Bush" cartoon of Bush in Superman costume; multicolor; 3 in.

Two Winners/The Yankees and George W. Bush" Championship New York Yankees baseball team symbol and bust of George W, multicolor; $1^1/4$ in.

"W Stands for Women/Bush 2000" slogan button; r, w; 2 in.

Anti-Bush

"Insider Trading" jugate portraits of Bush-Cheney with White House in b.g. and large red slash cross-out symbol supered over pictures; multicolor; $1^3/4$ in.

"Pants On Fire/Dump W/in 2004" cartoon of Bush wearing jersey with big "W; takeoff on "Liar, Liar" theme; multicolor: 2 in.

"Stop Mad Cowboy Disease"; cartoon of Bush wearing ten gallon cowboy hat; multicolor: 3 in.

Collector's Choice: 2000 Florida Recount

"'I Was There Gore? Bush' Nov. 9, 2000/Palm Beach Country Recount," jugate portrait; multicolor; 2 in.

"Wanted/Democratic Enemy No. 1 Secretary of the State of Florida"; photo of Katherine Harris who conducted recount; multicolor; 2 in.

"Wanted/Republican Enemy No. 1/" Carol Roberts, Member; Palm Beach Country Canvassing Board"; photo of Roberts; multicolor; 2 in.

"Thou Shalt not steal . . . or be a crybaby/Sore 2000 Loserman"; Smiling symbol with wearing frown; jugate of Gore-Lieberman; r, w, b, blk; 6 in.

"2000/The Gore-inch Who Tried to Steal the Election"; clever cartoon of Dr. Seuss's Grinch in Santa costume; r, gr, w, blk; $1^3/_4$ in.

Collector's Choice: Al Gore, Democratic nominee, 2000

"For California and the Nation" trigate; pictures Al Gore, Joe Lieberman and California 18th Dist. Congressman Gary Condit, running for reelection (Condit later was defeated after a moral impropriety), multicolor; 3 in.

" I Gave Mine/Gore 2000" map of Iowa with single drop of red blood supered over; indicated dedicated campaign workers' willingness to donate blood to the cause; issued after the 2000 Iowa caucus; r, w, blk; $2^1/_4$ in.

"Gore-Lieberman 2000, Alaska" sweeping star supered over state outline; r, w, b; $2^1/_4$ in.

"Join the Fight/Gore Super Tuesday March 7, 2000" primary button; map of the US with shooting star above Gore name; r, w, b; 2 in.

"Machinists Support Gore/Lieberman/District 57" slogan pin; intriguing design has Machinists Union logo as the "O" in Gore; r, w, b; $2^1/_4$ in.

"Moving Forward-Victory 2000" black silhouetted moving van with words "Lock Stock & Barrels/Nashville, Tennessee"; r, w, b; 2 in.

"The People/Not the Powerful" 2000 Gore's most potent slogan pin; r, w, b; 2^1/4 in.

"Women for Gore/Al Gore for President 2000/Together We Can Do It"; World War II's Rosie the Riveter redux; cartoon shows lady factory worker with sleeves rolled up flexing her muscles; w, blk; 9 in.

8

THE INSTANT
EXPERT QUIZ

1. What are buttons that feature a pair of political party candidates called?

2. The death of what president spurred the purposeful collecting of political artifacts?

3. According to dealer Dave Frent, the most intense competition in the hobby prevails in what price range?

4. In the section on sharpening your visual skills, what two top museums are cited?

5. What third-party candidate ranks among the favorite collecting specialties?

6. What are considered as the two prime sources for a wide variety of political artifacts?

7. What term, referring to "any cheaply contrived object," does the APIC use to denote reproductions and fantasies?

8. What two ex-presidential candidates helped enact the Hobby Protection Act in 1973 requiring that a bogus button is clearly marked as "Reproductions"?

9. Amanda Lougee's invention revolutionized the hobby in 1896. What was it?

10. Who was the first and foremost celluloid button manufacturer?

11. Fading of political buttons is caused by what major culprit?

12. What *Cause* buttons today represent the most imaginative and still underpriced specialty?

13. What year was the nineteenth amendment passed granting women the right to vote?

14. Who was the first black woman to run for president?

15. The name of what hate group, founded during Reconstruction, loosely translates from the Greek word kuklos?

16. What first lady acted in her husband's behalf in running the country during his six-month convalescence following a stroke?

17. Who was the first woman nominated on a major party ticket?

18. What popular kids TV favorite in the 1952 picked up more write-in votes than most third-party candidates?

19. What inaugural lapel items are esteemed as the scarcest and most desirable?

20. A McKinley lunchbox pin, rated among the hobby's Top 10, would be considered inappropriate today. Why?

Answers and Sources

1. A Jugate.—See *Glossary*.

2. Abraham Lincoln's assassination.—See *History of Collecting*.

3. The Smithsonian and Museum of American Political Life.—See *Finding Your Collecting Groove*.

4. The $50-100 range.—See *Finding Your Collecting Groove*.

5. Teddy Roosevelt, who ran on both GOP and Progressive tickets. Socialist Eugene Debs rates as another favorite.—See *Finding Your Collecting Groove*.

6. GOP and Democratic National Conventions; also Mail Auction and Fixed Price Catalogs.—See *On The Campaign Trail For Buttons*.

7. Brummagem—See *Detecting Fakes and Fantasies*.

8. Senators Barry Goldwater and George McGovern.—See *Detecting Fakes and Fantasies*.

9. The modern celluloid button.—See *Dawning of the Age of Amanda*.

10. Whitehead and Hoag.—See *Button Manufacturers and Jobbers*.

11. Sunlight or ultraviolet (UV) rays.—See *Housing and Showcasing Your Collection*.

12. 1960s Student Protest and Anti-War Movement.—See *All For The Cause Protest Groups*.

13. 1920, the year of the 34th presidential election—Harding vs. Coolidge. See *Woman's Suffrage*.

14. New York Congresswoman Shirley Chisholm in 1972.—See *Black History Memorabilia*.

15. Ku Klux Klan. See *Other Causes Heard From*.

16. Edith Galt Wilson, Woodrow Wilson's wife.—See *First Ladies*.

17. Geraldine Ferraro running as the vice presidential candidate on the ticket with Walter Mondale in 1984.—See *Lady Candidates*.

18. Howdy Doody, as part of an NBC promotion.—See *Hopefuls*.

19. 1789, 1792 George Washington clothing buttons.—See *Inaugurals*.

20. McKinley "Do You Smoke? Yes, Since 1896" button. Shows busy factory smokestacks spewing smoke. Pollution imagery would be a turnoff for environmentalists.—See *A Portfolio of Blue Ribbon Winners*.

RESOURCE GUIDE

GLOSSARY

Acetate
A clear synthetic layer derived from ester of cellulose. Noted for a virtually light-reflective surface. Typically featured in World War II vintage pinbacks.

Acronyms and abbreviations
Beginning in the mid-1930s with Franklin Roosevelt's numerous programs, NRA, WPA, OPA, etc., acronyms became popular as a kind of shorthand for presidents and other candidates as well. Roosevelt himself was referred to more familiarly as FDR, Harry Truman, HST, John Kennedy , JFK, Lyndon Johnson, LBJ, Hubert Humphrey, HHH, and most recently, George W. Bush, simply W. The Grand Old Party is invariably the GOP.

Albumen
Combination of egg whites serving as a binder with silver salts; originated in the mid-nineteenth century and in the US paper photographic print; featured in presidential portraiture and on political lapel devices; invariably sepia in color. Popular as late as the 1870s.

Altered
A pinback ribbon medallion recognizable in one form, which has been transformed or "doctored" by devious entrepreneurs to capitalize on what might appear to be a new find in the hobby. Another fake, the *repin*, might mate a legitimate back paper with a newer button produced after the fact, using modern materials.

Amalgam
Paper on tin or celluloid. Any of a variety of alloys of mercury, usually brass, sandwiched together to form political shell badges.

Ambrotype

A positive photo on glass, backed by dark color; had its major impact in the 1860s presidential race but soon lost out to paper print images.

Back-papers

Messages or company logos printed directly on the reverse of lithograph buttons. This designated them as reproductions in compliance with the Hobby Protection Act. Unscrupulous wheeler dealers, however, have been known to remove back-printing ink with solvents in an attempt to pass off an item as original. The promotional GMC and Kleenex repro series of 1968, and the Crackerbarrel set of 1972 are noted examples of back printing.

Bartenders Delight

Pinback depicting candidates from rival parties as a token of impartiality. Advertisers often produced them and button manufacturers often provided them as salesmen's samples; also known as "Salesman's Safety Pins."

Browntone

Lighter shade or texture of brown in a photograph or illustration popular on pinbacks in the late nineteenth century, replacing the sepiatone.

Brummagen (Brum'-i-Jem)

An archaic form of the name Birmingham, the English city notorious as hotbed for counterfeit coins in the seventeenth century. Term applies in the hobby to any cheaply contrived object, having a showy quality, but a reproduction and not the genuine article. (See *"How to Detect Fakes and Fantasies."*)

Button

Term used interchangeably with pinbacks or lapel pins. The term should not be confused with clothing or uniform buttons—a field of collecting in itself.

Celluloid

or cello (sell-o). Generic term for pinbacks featuring clear plastic-like layer of protective coating over paper or metal disks; reflects light unevenly. Common button material from 1896 to 1920. A few solid celluloid lapel pins are known for Grover Cleveland, James Blaine, Rutherford Hayes, Samuel Tilden and Benjamin Harrison.

Centerpiece

or cornerstone. Usually applies to an oversize, dynamic pinback, medallion or paper hanger that stands out in a grouping or special display of political items. Convention and inaugural buttons from the 1960s often are found in six- through nine-inch sizes, including those featuring Dewey, Truman, Reagan, Eisenhower, Nixon.

Clasp-back

As the name implies, a locking catch or clasp that firmly locks-in pin as an option to the more common spring wire-pin.

1896 "Bartender's Delight" gives option of William Bryan or William McKinley depending how you turn image inside phonograph horn.

Classic

An aesthetically appealing political item that clearly exemplifies a given campaign, regardless of rarity.

Coattail

Any button that names or pictures a top political slate (president and vice president) with image of a nominee as a way of boosting his or her run for a lower office (i.e., senator, governor).

Collet

The inner metal ring or collar on a button that locks the celluloid disk into the paper or metal.

Curl

The rim or ridge, not visible head on, between outer edge of the face and collet. Union labels (known as bugs), logos and other identifying marks often appear on curl.

Daguerreotype

Invented in 1839 and became first presidential photographs to appear on lapel devices; introduced in the 1848 campaign of Zachary Taylor. Dags, highly prized by photophiles, were popular from 1843 to 1855, subsequently replaced by ferrotypes.

Fantasy

A term coined by Ted Hake of Hake's Americana in the 1960s to apply to a newly-created item that was unauthorized or never existed, but gives the appearance of dating from an earlier time period. A notable early fantasy picturing John Fremont, the party's first presidential nominee, was issued by the National Republican League to commemorate the GOP's 50th anniversary in 1906.

Ferrotype
A lapel device with brass or cloth covered frame containing a tintype image of a candidate.

Flasher
Plastic lapel pin, usually three inches in diameter, that shows a presidential candidate's image when tilted one way and his running mate or a related image when tilted at another angle. First used in the Eisenhower vs. Stevenson campaign in the 1950s.

Foxing
One of the biggest enemies of celluloid pinbacks, is a brown stain caused by moisture rusting the metal rim and encroaching under the celluloid layer.

Jugate (Joo-gat)
Images of a pair of party candidates, most notably the top slate. Whether on pinbacks, banners or posters, jugates are hotly pursued.

Key Item
An elite artifact, most often a pinback, that ranks in the top five percent among collectors in terms of rarity, desirability and graphic impact.

Lithograph
Campaign lapel devices stamped from tin and printed directly on its surface. This less-expensive device took over from the cellos in the early 1920s. Lithograph is also a generic used by collectors when referring to prints, posters and broadsides.

Lithopane
A semi-transparent porcelain plaque with incised design or image appearing in varying thicknesses. When backlit, thick areas restrict light and tin areas transmit light, creating a dramatic, colorful effect. Lithopanes are found as lamp shades and fireplace screens, but most commonly appeared in windows, much the same as stained glass.

Their popularity spanned from 1850 to 1870, with superb specimens known for candidates Henry Clay, Winfield Scott and Zachary Taylor.

Litho Under Glass

Engraved paper portrait of leading candidates appearing under a glass disk is secured in pewter frame. First known campaign example is for 1828 Andrew Jackson-John Quincy Adams tilt. Early versions featured small mirror on reverse with brass loop atop frame suitable for hanging as wall plaque. Later versions depicted the vice-presidential candidate on the reverse. By the 1848 John Tyler-Lewis Cass race, interest in this medium had waned.

Medal

A political numismatics term for issues ranging in diameter from $1^3/4$ to approximately 3 inches. Used interchangeably with *medallion*, which measures slightly larger with a $2^1/2$ to over 3 inch range. A *medalet* is slightly smaller, measuring up to $1^3/4$ inches.

Multicolor

Term used in the hobby to denote any full-color items; portraits may often even include flesh tones.

Name Button

Pinback featuring one or more candidate's names, dates, nicknames or initials; e.g. "Roosevelt-1912"; "Harding and Coolidge."

Novelty button

First used as attention-getters on lapel devices in the late 1960s and 1970s novelties with plastic jiggley eyes and other moving features, as well as lights and music (via a computer chip), have enjoyed limited popularity.

Patch Box

Novel little container, usually of pasteboard and glass resembling a miniature book; so called because it held tiny cosmetic (rouge or powder) patches favored by ladies in the early nineteenth century. Candidates' portraits often appeared on the glass lid, although most were probably commemorative rather than campaign oriented.

Pinback

A common term for modern campaign lapel device, usually featuring a spring wire-pin.

Planchet

A flat metal disk that takes the engraving or stamping of a pinback design.

Rebus Button

A favorite among collectors known for clever juxtaposition or play on words using pictures and symbols to punch out a slogan or name of a favorite nominee, e.g., a 1912 "I Wood Row Wilson," picturing Wilson and running mate Thomas Marshall being rowed in a boat with White House in background; a 1936 "Land-On Washington," with Alf Landon leaning out of an airplane as it circles Capitol dome.

Ribbon

Pioneered as simple strips of printed cloth attached to lapels with pins in Jacksonian era; enjoyed greatest popularity from 1876 to 1892 with over 600 varieties documented. Ribbons evolved as highly elaborate silk specimens in festive colors and gold or silver lettering.

Ribbon Badge

A highly-desirable political ribbon to which a medal or button is attached or suspended; popularized at national party conventions, parades, presidential inaugurations and other galas and special events.

Shank Button

Clothing button with metal loop on reverse through which thread is passed to attach to wearer's sleeve or lapel. Notable examples were the George Washington Inaugurals of 1789 and 1792.

Slogan Buttons

Items bearing an often alliterative political maxim or directive; e.g., "We Need Adlai Badly" Stevenson, 1960; "Truman Fights for Human Rights," HST 1948; "Keep Cool with Coolidge," Calvin Coolidge, 1924.

Stanhope

A miniature celluloid or ivory telescope containing images of party candidates. A stunning example from the Grover Cleveland race shows his portrait by peering into the end of a an ornate ivory fountain pen. In the guise of figural animals in white metal, these clever novelties offered less flattering magnified views of politicos, as observed through the rear end of a pig.

Stickpin
Metal or celluloid button with attached pin up to 2 inches long to wear in lapel, hat, or necktie.

Stud
Small ornamental button mounted on a short post for insertion through an eyelet on items of clothing. Also known as tie tacks. Favorites include the 1952 Adlai Stevenson tiny gold shoe with a hole in it, the Kennedy PT-109 Boat, 1960, and the Walter Mondale die-cut state studs of 1976.

Sulfide
Cameo visualization of a candidate or party symbol set on an enameled surface; enjoyed a vogue in campaign brooches in Andrew Jackson, Martin Van Buren and William Henry Harrison races. Other prized sulfide incarnations included paperweights, doorknobs and perfume bottles. Sulfide playing marbles are known with imbedded busts of Theodore Roosevelt, William McKinley, Grover Cleveland and William Howard Taft.

Tab
Flat die-cut metal piece bearing picture or slogan with fold-over flap (or tab) that secures it to lapel or pocket. One of the least pricey and readily obtainable campaign items, tabs have gained a loyal following.

Threadboxes
Probably the first real campaign items issued, and ironically intended for the distaff side, even though women were denied the right to vote at the time. Imported from France originally and made of pasteboard in gilt trim with sides of rainbow-hued paper and velvet pincushion atop lid, the boxes contained a glass enclosed paper engraving of the candidate inside the hinged cover. Extremely uncommon, thread boxes are known for the John Quincy Adams-Andrew Jackson campaigns of 1824 and 1828

Three-Dimensional
Any politically-related item having more than two sides including statuary, glassware, ceramics, toys and parade canes.

Token

Numismatic issue used as a monetary substitute e.g., the Hard Times tokens picturing Andrew Jackson, among others from the 1830s.

Trigate

Three images of candidates on a single button, nominally the president, vice president and a coattail candidate. A *quadragate* features four candidates; a *multigate* more than four.

BIBLIOGRAPHY

Political Lapel Devices

Albert, Adolpheus H., *Record of American Uniform and Historical Buttons with Supplement*. Hightstown, NJ; Author; 1973.

Cobb, J. Herold, *George Washington Inaugural Buttons and Medalets: 1789 and 1793;* Privately printed 1963.

DeWitt, J. Doyle, *A Century of Campaign Buttons: 1789-1889*, Hartford, CT; Privately printed, 1959.

Hake, Ted, *The Encyclopedia of Political Buttons Book I-1896-1972*, printed 1974;*Book II-1920-1976*, printed 1977; *Book III-1789-1916*, printed 1978 NY, Dafran House Publishers. All three encyclopedias are available, as well as price updates from Ted Hake, P.O. Box 1444, York, PA 17405-1444.

Sigoloff, Marc, *Collecting Political Buttons*, Chicago Review Press, 1988.

Sullivan, Edmund S. *American Political Badges and Medalets/1789-1892*, Lawrence, MA, Quartermain Publications, 1981. Revised edition of J. Doyle Dewitt's *A Century of Campaign Buttons, 1789-1889.*

General Political Memorabilia

Roger A. Fischer, *Tippecanoe and Trinkets Too*, University of Chicago Press, 1988.

Friz, Richard, *The Official Price Guide to Political Memorabilia*, House of Collectibles, New York, 1988.

Fratkin, Robert, *Political Souvenirs: Reminders of Old Campaigns*, The Encyclopedia of Collectibles, Vol. P-Q, pp.64-75; Alexandria, VA, Time-Life Books, 1979.

Gores, Stan, *Presidential and Campaign Memorabilia*, Second Edition, Wallace Homestead Book Company, 1988.

Hake, Ted, *Hake's Guide to Presidential Campaign Collectibles*, Wallace Homestead Co, Radnor, Pennsylvania, 1992.

Kenneth C. Melder, *Hail to the Candidate/Presidential Campaigns from Banners to Broadcasts*, Smithsonian Press, Washington, D.C., 1992.

Sullivan, Edmund S., *Collecting Political Americana*, Crown Publishers, NY, 1980.

Wagner, Dale, *Presidential Campaign Memorabilia: A Concise History, 1789-1972*, Public Policy Research Associates, Washington, D.C. 1972.

Warda, Mark, *100 Years of Political Campaign Collectibles*, Galt Press, Clearwater Florida,1996.

Wearin, Otha D., *Political Americana/The Story of Political Gadgets and Push Buttons*,World Publishing Co., Shenandoah, IA, 1967.

POLITICAL LIBRARIES AND MUSEUMS

American Antiquarian Society
185 Salisbury St.
Worcester, MA 01609

Clark Historical Library
Central Michigan University
Mt. Pleasant, MI 48804

Library of Congress
101 Independence Ave. SE
Washington D.C. 20600
(202) 707-5000
www.loc.gov

Museum of American Political Life
University of Hartford
West Hartford, CT 06101

National Archives and Records
7th and Pennsylvania Ave. N NW
Washington D.C. 20600
(202) 501-5000 or 1-866-325-7208
www.archives.gov

National Museum of History and Technology
Smithsonian Institution,
Smithsonian National Mall
900 Jefferson Drive
Washington D.C. 20600

New Hampshire Historical Society Manuscripts Library
(N. H. Primary-related memorabilia)
30 Park St.
Concord, NH 33301
(603) 228-6688 or 856-0610
www.nhhistory.org

Paul Perlin Collection of Political Americana
University of Louisville
Louisville, KY 40232

The Presidential Museum
622 N. Lee
Odessa, TX 79761

Partisan Prohibition Historical Society
Needmore, PA, 17238
www.prohibitionists.org

Western Reserve Historical Society
Cleveland, OH 44101

Wisconsin State Historical Society
Madison, WI 53714

MEMORIAL FOUNDATIONS HONORING SPECIFIC PRESIDENTS AND NATIONAL SHRINES DEDICATED TO PRESIDENTS

Of the Presidential Libraries listed below, all except the Nixon Library which is private, are coordinated by the National Archives Records Administration. NARA also has custody of the Nixon presidential historic documents and those of Bill Clinton. NARA will release Clinton records to the public at the newly-completed Clinton Library beginning Jan.20, 2006. All materials for presidents prior to Herbert Hoover are held by private institutions.

George H.W. Bush Library
1000 George Bush Drive West
College Station, Texas
Phone: (979) 691-4000
E-Mail: library.bush@nara.gov
Website: www.bushlibrary.tamu.edu

Jimmy Carter Library
441 Freedom Pkwy.
Atlanta, Georgia 30307-1496
Phone: (404) 331-3942
E-Mail: *carter.library*.nara.gov
Website: www.jimmycarterlibrary.org

Calvin Coolidge State Park and Museum
Plymouth Notch, VT
Phone: (802) 672-3773
Website: www.historic.vermont.org

William J. Clinton Library
100 La Harpe Blvd.
Little Rock, AR 72201
Phone: (501) 244-9756
E-Mail: clinton.library.@nara.gov
Website: www.clinton.archives.gov

Dwight D. Eisenhower National Historic Site
Gettysburg, PA 17325

Dwight D. Eisenhower Library
200 S.E. 4th. St.
Abilene, KS 67410-2900
Phone: (785) 263-4571:
1-800-Ring Ike
E-Mail:
eisenhower.library@nara.gov
Website:
www.eisenhower.archives.gov

Gerald R. Ford Library
1000 Beal Ave.
Ann Arbor, MI 48109-2114
Phone: (734) 205-0555
E-Mail: ford.library@nara.gov
Website: www.fordutexas.edu

General Grant Monument and Museum (a.k.a. Grant's Tomb)
26 Wall St.
New York, NY 10001
Phone: (212) 666 1640

President Benjamin Harrison Foundation
Indianapolis, IN 46206

Herbert Hoover Presidential Library
210 Parkside Drive, Box 488
West Branch, IA 52358-9685
Phone : (319) 643-5301
E-Mail: hoover.library@nara.gov
Website: www.hoover.archives.gov

Illinois State Historical Library (Lincolniana)
Springfield, Illinois 62703

Lyndon Baines Johnson Library
2313 Red River St.
Austin, TX 78705-5072
Phone: (512) 721-0200
E-Mail: johnson.library@nara.gov
Website: www.lbjib.utexas.edu

John F. Kennedy National Historic Site (birthplace)
83 Beal Street
Brookline, MA 02446
Phone: (617) 566-7937

JFK Memorial Library and Museum
Columbia Point Road
Boston, MA, 02125-3398
Phone: (617) 514-1600;
(866) J FK-1960
E-Mail: kennedy.library@nara.gov
Website: www.jfklibrary.org

Richard M. Nixon Library and Birthplace
18001 Yorba Linda Blvd.
Yorba Linda, CA 92886
Phone: (714) 993-5075
E-Mail: archives@nara.gov
Website: www.nixonfoundation.org

Ronald Reagan Library
40 Presidential Drive
Simi Valley, CA 93065-0600
Phone: (800) 410-8354
E-Mail: reagan.library@nara.gov
Website: www.reagan.utexas.edu

Franklin D. Roosevelt Library
4079 Albany Post Rd.
Hyde Park, NY 12538-1990
Phone: (845) 486-7770;
(800) FDR-Visit
E-Mail: roosevelt.library@nara.gov
Website: www.fdrlibrary.marist.edu

Theodore Roosevelt Association
Sagamore Hill National Historical
Site
Cove Neck Road
Oyster Bay, NY
(516) 922-4447

**William Howard Taft National
Historic Site**
2038 Auburn Road
Cincinnati, OH 45219-3028
(513) 684-3262

Harry S. Truman Library
500 West St. U.S. Hwy. 24
Independence, MO 64050-2481
Phone: (816) 833-1400;
(800) 833-1225
E-Mail: truman.library@nara.gov
Website: www.trumanlibrary.org

Woodrow Wilson House
2340 NW,
Washington D.C. 20600
(202) 387-4062

SHRINES TO PRESIDENTS

Ford's Theater (Abraham Lincoln)
Washington, D.C. 20600

**Thomas Jefferson National
Historic Site**
Monticello, VA

**Abraham Lincoln Birthplace
National Historic Site,**
Rte. 1, Hodgenville, KY 42748

**John Jay Library (Houses the
John D. Rockefeller McClellan-
Lincoln Collection)**
Brown University
20 Prospect Street
Providence, RI 02912

**Lincoln Memorial University
Carnegie Library**
(American Lincoln Center for Lin-
coln Studies)
Harrogate, TN 37752

**Lincoln-Warren Jones Lincoln
Collection**
Louisiana State University
Baton Rouge, LA 70803

**Butler University Irwin Library
(Charles W. Moore Lincoln
Collection)**
4600 Sunset Ave.
Indianapolis, IN 46208

**Lincoln—Harold Sage Lincoln
Collection**
Illinois State University,
Miller Library
Normal, IL 61761

**Lincoln Memorial Shrine Smiley
Public Library**
125 West Vine St.
Redlands, CA 92373
(one of the largest Lincoln memorabilia collections in the country)

**Abraham Lincoln Tomb Historic
Site, Oak Ridge Cemetery**
Springfield, IL 62703
1-800-545-7300

**Smith College (Women's Suffrage
Collection)**
Northampton, MA 01060

U.S. Military Academy
(Archive including generals who
became president from U.S. Grant
to Eisenhower)
West Point, NY 10996

**George Washington Mt. Vernon
National Monument**
Mt. Vernon, VA 22121
(703) 780-2000
www.mountvernon.org
Mail-Phone Auctioneers
The following hold mail/phone
auctions and or fixed price catalog
auctions:

DIRECT MAIL-PHONE AUCTIONEERS

Al Anderson Auctions
P.O. Box 644
Troy, Ohio 45373
(937) 339-0850
aauctnerinet.com

David Frent, Political Americana Auction
Oakhurst, New Jersey 07755
(732) 922-0768
PolAmerl@aol.com

Ted Hake, Americana and Collectibles
P.O. Box 1444
York, Pennsylvania 17405-1444
(717) 848-1333
auction@hakes.com

Tom French
P.O. Box 1755
Capitola, California 95010
(831) 476-6850
tomfrench77@acl.com

Slater's American, Inc. and
Slater's Provenance Auction
5335 North Tacoma Ave. Suite 24,
Indianapolis, Indiana 46220
(317) 257-3044
www.slatersamericana.com

Rex Stark, Americana
P.O. Box 1029
Gardner, Massachusetts 01440
(978) 630-3237
rexstark@yahoo.com

POLITICAL COLLECTING ORGANIZATIONS

American Political Items Collectors (APIC)
P.O. Box 5632
Derwood, MD 20855-0632.
E-Mail: info@apic.us.
There are 21 Specialty Chapters
and 26 Geographical Chapters

in the APIC. Names and addresses, Chapter contacts, though subject to change, are listed in the current APIC Roster Handbook, Section III.

Geographical
Arizona Political Collectors

Big Apple Ed Potter

Chicago Area (CAPIC)

Mac McGraw/Colorado Pol. Items Collector

Dakota Territy Chapter

J. Doyle DeWitt–Connecticut

Dixie (Southeast)

Florida

Gateway to the West (St. Louis)

Indiana

Pol. Amer. Coll. of Kentucky

Mason Dixon (PA/MD)

Michigan

Mid-Atlantic

Missouri Valley

Monroe D. Ray-Empire (NY)

National Capital Area

North Star (MN)

Northern California

Northern New England

Ohio

Oregon

Southern California

Southwest

Washington State Political Items Collectors

Wisconsin

Specialty Chapters
American Locals Pol. Items Coll.

APIC Cause Chapter

APIC Labor History Chapter

Bush Pol. Items Coll.

Carter Pol. Items Coll.

Democratic Political Items Collectors

Gerald R. Ford

The Al Gore Chapter

The 3-H Chapter-Hubert Humphrey

Kennedy Chapter

The Rail-Splitter (Lincoln) Chapter

Ronald Reagan Chapter

Republican Pol. Items Coll.

Franklin D. Roosevelt Chapter

Theodore Roosevelt Chapter

Third Party and Hopeful Chapter

Harry S Truman

Wendell Willkie Chapter

Women's Suffrage and Political Issues Chapter

INDEX